AF574322

Water

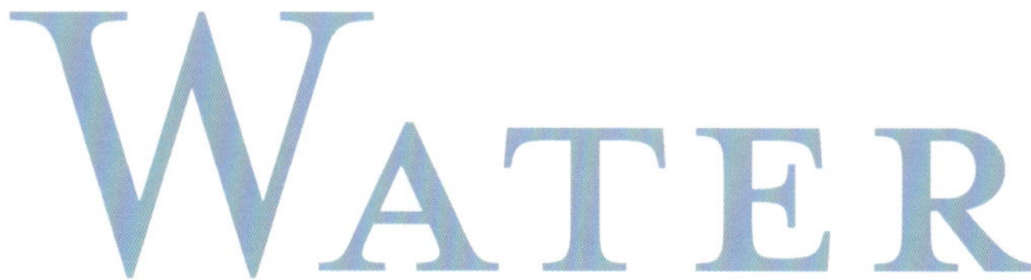

Lawren Harris and the Group of Seven

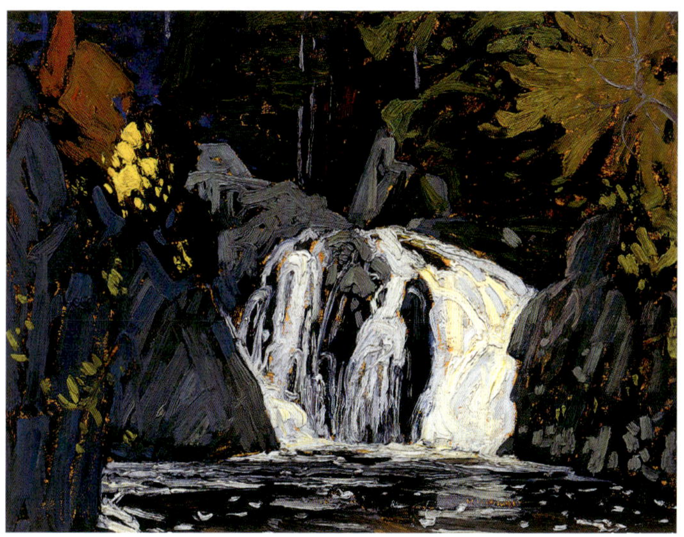

Joan Murray

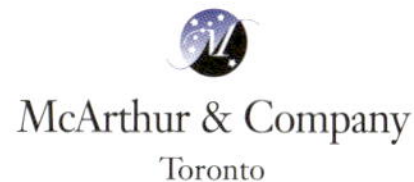

McArthur & Company
Toronto

Published in Canada in 2004 by
McArthur & Company
322 King Street West, Suite 402
Toronto, Ontario
M5V 1J2
www.mcarthur-co.com

Library and Archives Canada Cataloguing in Publication

Murray, Joan
Water : Lawren Harris and the Group of Seven / Joan Murray.

ISBN 1-55278-457-6

1. Harris, Lawren, 1885–1970. 2. Group of Seven (Group of artists)
3. Water in art. I. Title.

ND249.H36M88 2004 759.11 C2004-904238-6

Front jacket photograph: *North Shore, Lake Superior*, National Gallery of Canada
Back jacket photograph: *Spring Rapids*, National Gallery of Canada
Title page photograph: *Agawa Waterfall*, The Thomson Collection

Design and composition by Counterpunch
Printed in Canada by Friesens

The publisher would like to acknowledge the financial support of the Government of Canada through the Book Publishing Industry Development Program, the Canada Council, and the Ontario Arts Council for our publishing activities. We also acknowledge the Government of Ontario through the Ontario Media Development Corporation Ontario Book Initiative.

10 9 8 7 6 5 4 3 2 1

"We found Algoma a rugged, wild land packed with an amazing variety of subjects. It was a veritable paradise for the creative adventures in paint in the Canadian north."

Lawren Harris, *The Story of the Group of Seven*, page 19

Contents

Unknown photographer, Montreal River, Algoma –
a photograph obtained by J.E.H. MacDonald in 1918
Thoreau MacDonald collection, courtesy of a private collector

Just Add Water

The craggy hills, covered with tall trees, towered against the blue sky. The man climbed, now listening to the leaves crunch beneath his feet, now stepping on thick, springy cushions of moss. He took in the deep golden green of the leaves, the brown undergrowth – and then, from the top of the hill, he saw the Montreal River winding down below him into hills that dropped steeply to Lake Superior. What he especially loved to paint were waterfalls, and he sang as he did so – with the rushing water an accompaniment. In his heart, he felt uneasy with all the beauty of the place, as though he had come to a home too lavish for his taste. There it was, right enough – the Montreal River – in this remote location in Algoma in Canyon, 182 kilometres north of Sault Ste. Marie. Lawren Harris peered again at the water.

This was no chance encounter. It was one of the great events in the three-week trip Harris had organized in the fall of 1919. Since the country offered no place to stay for him and his friends, who included J.E.H. MacDonald, Harris had arranged for the use of a boxcar on the Algoma Central Railway fitted up with bunks, sink, and stove. At three places, the railway left the freight car on a siding: first and most northerly at Canyon, second at Hubert, and third at Batchawana. Since the spring of 1918, Harris had been travelling to Algoma with their mutual friend, Dr. J.M. MacCallum, a great art patron as well as a specialist in ophthalmology. The autumn of 1918 was the first time that he had been accompanied on a boxcar excursion by MacDonald, along with Frank Johnston. Now, in September 1919, Harris made the trip again. This time A.Y. Jackson, another of their painting peers, joined the crew.

How glad Harris was that he had organized this trip. Early in 1918, he had had a nervous breakdown caused by dismay over his work in the First World War as a gunnery teacher at Camp Borden. The shock of two terrible deaths – his friend Tom Thomson in 1917 and his beloved younger brother, Howard, killed in action in February 1918 – led to more despair. Harris's breakdown had terrifying symptoms: "troublous" sleep as he described it, terrified tossings and turnings, and a panicky feeling that made him awaken with a start. He was confused, disoriented, and – worse for his optimistic personality – he felt that all he had built was on sand.[1]

By May 1918, he had recovered enough energy to make a convalescent trip to Algoma in Northern Ontario, accompanied by Dr. MacCallum. It was a distant region and the only way to reach it was to take the Algoma Central Railway. Harris later described the area as a "rugged wild land packed with an amazing variety of subjects."[2] For him, it was a veritable paradise. Algoma, he could see, was a country that afforded a broad, rich treatment, one that combined the idea of wilderness and virgin nature with vast resource potential.

Harris soon found that he was able to sketch again. His first trip to Algoma helped strengthen his constitution and clear his mind. Now, in 1919, on his second trip, he was feeling much better and as a result, travelling farther afield. Ever since he attended high school in Toronto, he had delighted in sports. At the school, St. Andrew's College in Rosedale, he had become a strong swimmer and diver. Water was a way of tuning in to health for him and of responding to the harsh surface-beauty of life. As his friend F.B. Housser described it, Algoma was a place slashed by ravines and canyons through which ran rivers, streams, and springs broadening into lakes, and it gave Harris such a feeling of elation that he told MacDonald it recalled the "original site of the Garden of Eden."[3]

Algoma was wild; it was forested; it was hilly; and from it a great river flowed, a river that had made a startling difference to Canadian history. It seemed to Harris the source of the first human life, of God's country, of paradise.

The word "paradise" derives from the Persian word for a "royal pleasure garden." In the Bible, Eden is described as an abundant garden. In the Algoma paintings of Harris and his friends, paradise is imagined as a place of rich and flowing waters. In the biblical story of paradise, man and nature are in harmony – all are imagined as being at peace. The scene is sometimes shown in art as similar to the ideal reign of Arcadia in ancient Greece, the domain of Pan, the god of nature and a wild creature.

Harris wished to evoke not only paradise but also Arcadia in his work. He was familiar with Romantic poets such as Percy Bysshe Shelley to whom nature expressed something larger and nobler than human life: natural beauty seemed to express that to Harris, too. But more than that, going north, Harris felt that he had gone backwards in time. Going upriver, he had approached what to him was the source – of life, and certainly of art. It seemed to him a special place on earth that played a central role in a flow of energy throughout creation, almost as though it were a way of levering wilderness throughout the rest of Canada, even the urban centres. He painted it this way, filled with power, combining the momentum of its waters with images of the huge granite rocks that covered the area and the rich colour of the fall season.

MacDonald described the country as dramatic, as a land suited to the poet Dante Alighieri. MacDonald spoke for Harris, in a way, when he expressed their feelings about the place to his wife, Joan, in one of his letters of September 1918. He described the canyon in which they were situated as being:

> like a winding way to the lower regions & last night, when the train went through just at dusk, with the fireman stoking up, the light of the fire stirring on the smoke clouds, it was easy to imagine his Satanic majesty taking a drive through his domain. I had walked a little distance up the canyon, and the effect was eerie enough to make me speed up for home. The great perpendicular rocks seemed to over-

> hang as though they might fall any minute & the dark Agawa moving quietly through it all had an uncanny snakiness. But yesterday was a dull & rainy day. On a fine day, such as this, the canyon seems to lead *upwards*, and has all the attributes of an imagined Paradise, excepting perhaps anything in the way of meadows. There are beautiful waterfalls on all sides & the finest trees, spruce, elm & pine. It is a Shelly like kind of place...the most impressive sight I have had on this trip was a view of lake Superior from a place about eight miles from here, on the way up. The railway is there within about 4 miles of the lake & probably 1500 feet above it, commanding a wonderful view of craggy hills, waterfalls & the winding Agawa. I have never seen anything so impressive, as the half-revealed extensiveness of the lake. It certainly was Superior in all ways. There was a haziness in the air which merged the horizon with the sky & that smooth glimmering infinity of waters was like a glimpse of God himself....It reminds one of Paul, being caught up & hearing unutterable things. (See page 124 in the Appendix for the full text of this letter.)[4]

For both Harris and MacDonald, the landscape was a heroic image, which suggested the country's origin in the northern wilderness. Harris's reaction to the scene before him led him to create one of his most important early paintings, *Waterfall, Algoma*, and to return to the subject again in *Algoma Waterfall* around 1926 (see pages 47 and 57). Harris's paintings are as important as MacDonald's fiery canvases, *The Wild River* (1919), *Falls, Montreal River* (1920), and *Algoma Waterfall* (1920) (see pages 95–97).

These paintings always startle: to look at them is to study where recorded art history, truth, and fiction meet. *Waterfall, Algoma* conveys Harris's remarkable painterly gifts to endow the scene before him with both immediacy and the timeless power of myth (see page 47). He makes palpable the power of the land he recorded and makes palpable, too, the mixture of rock

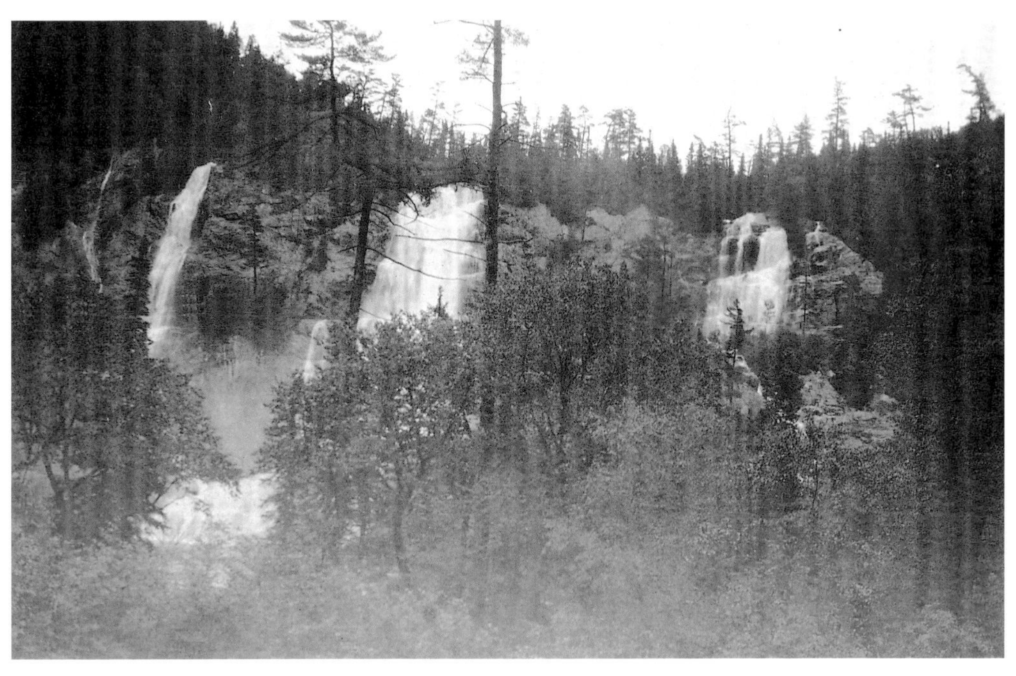

Falls, Montreal River, Algoma
Thoreau MacDonald collection, courtesy of a private collector

and water that was so much a part of the scene, delineating it with fervour and fidelity. The sketch of Harris's *Agawa Waterfall* is a tribute to the ideal of water (see page 43). It shows us the typical Harris space, which involves water as an interweaving of prospect and refuge. The forms of the water, which seems to stream towards us in the foreground, and the rocks and distant trees in the background give a dynamic but unified shape to the tension caused by the waterfall itself. The relationship between the shapes is what matters: the water, the trees, the distance, the observer, and the observed. Typically, he used the sketch to create his great painting *Algoma Waterfall* later, now emphasizing the unity that arose from the articulation of differences among the parts and the area's dark mystery (see page 57).

In Harris's many paintings of water, images of immense clarity contend with a sense of infinite space. By painting water, even frozen in the form of ice, he absorbed feelings, conflicts, impulses, and confusion. Watery, reflective surfaces, richly coloured skylines, wavy cutout forms, a restricted palette, smooth brushwork, a suggestive use of light – Harris's painting devices are concise and functional elements with which he pondered the philosophy that guided him. His methods go far towards explaining why we regard him as the architect of the Group of Seven. His design process involved impeccable clarity in analyzing relationships developed from forms: through them he referred to their original physical context and to private space situated in another time, another place.

There was the excitement too, generated by the boxcar trips, of a new community of artists. It was a period of tremendous creative ferment among the painters, who were to become the Group of Seven in 1920. Jackson, who joined the group on the trip in the autumn of 1919, also wrote enthusiastically about their time together to a friend, describing the view from a nearby hill where one could look over miles of primeval forest, as having spruce, balsam, and pine, and birches "you couldn't get your arms around."[5]

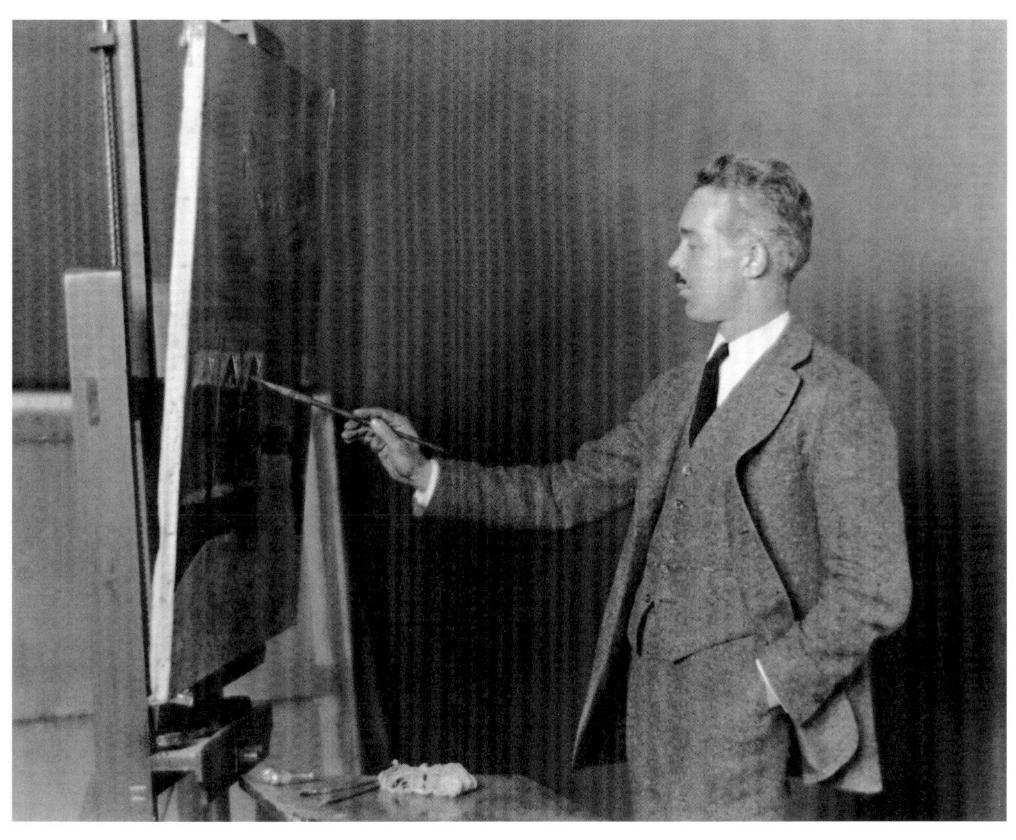

Lawren Harris painting in the Studio Building, c. 1920
National Gallery of Canada Library and Archives, Ottawa. 33190

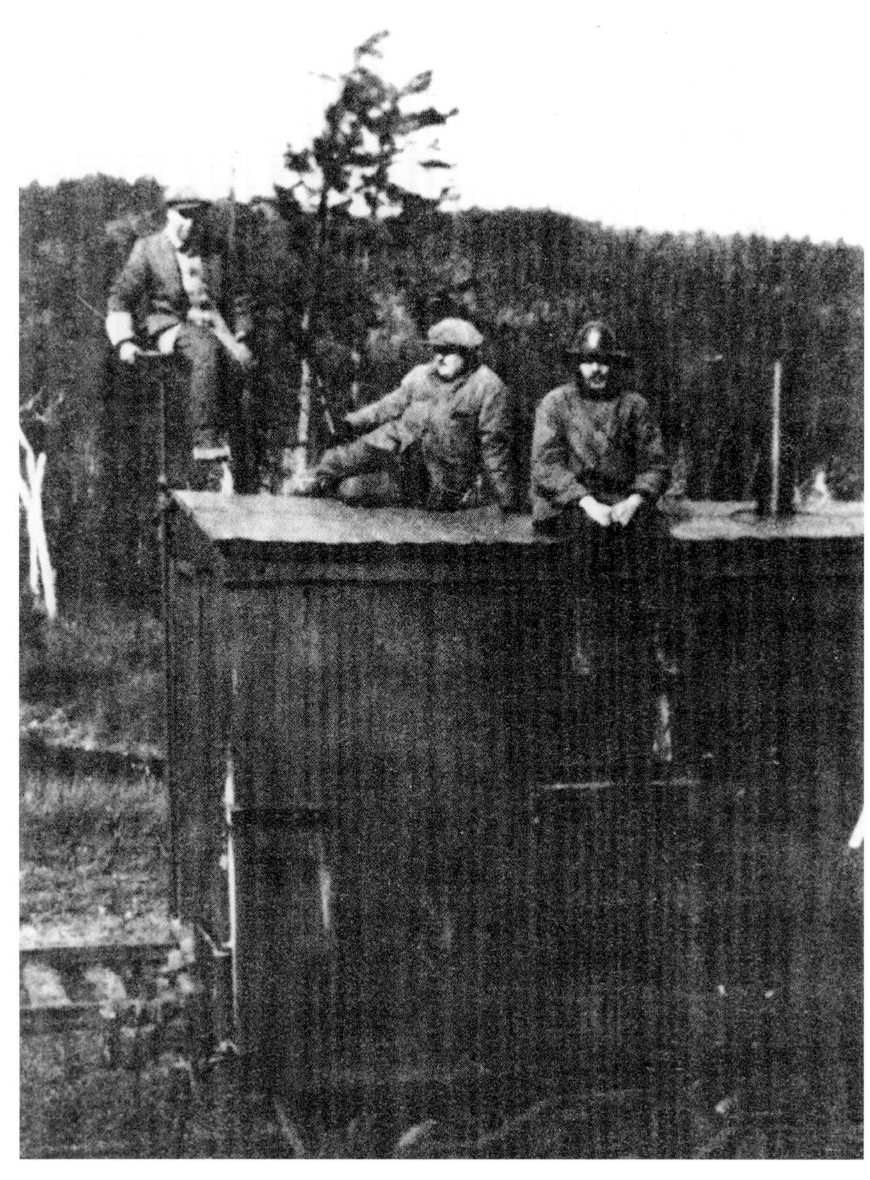

A.Y. Jackson, Frank Johnston, and Lawren Harris on A.C.R. 10557 in 1919 or 1920
McMichael Canadian Art Collection, Kleinburg

Comradeship and discussion were stimulating to the painting of these men. Later, Jackson recalled:

> The nights were frosty, but in the box car, with the fire in the stove, we were snug and warm. Discussions and arguments would last until late in the night, ranging from Plato to Picasso, to Madame Blavatsky and Mary Baker Eddy. Harris, a Baptist who later became a theosophist, and MacDonald, a Presbyterian who was interested in Christian Science, inspired many of the arguments. Outside, the aurora played antics in the sky, and the murmur of the rapids or a distant waterfall blended with the silence of the night."[6]

MacDonald also wrote extensively about the trip. In 1919, in an affectionate memoir published in *The Lamps*, the magazine of the Toronto Arts & Letters Club, he described the exterior look of the newly painted red boxcar A.C.R. 10557.[7] It had a "stiff little Xmas Tree" stuck in the top of the entrance ladder by the middle door and a moose skull below the window on the other side of the door: "This was topped with sprays of evergreen and red berries and had a design painted behind it including the motto, 'Ars Longa, Vita Brevis,' and a monogram made of the name letters of the crew of the car. Further along the side hung an old snowshoe of solid wood and an ancient shovel which might have been used to turn the first rock on the road."[8]

Inside, human disorder was kept within bounds by "J" (we don't know if this initial meant Jackson or Johnston), "who made the bed almost regularly," and by "H" (surely Harris), who "wielded a mighty morning broom down the middle passage between the piled up bunks."[9] There were two ways of travelling: by a railway "pede" (a three-wheeled jigger worked by hand) supplied for short runs on the track, and by canoe. The artists on the pede travelled down the track until "some attractive composition of spruce

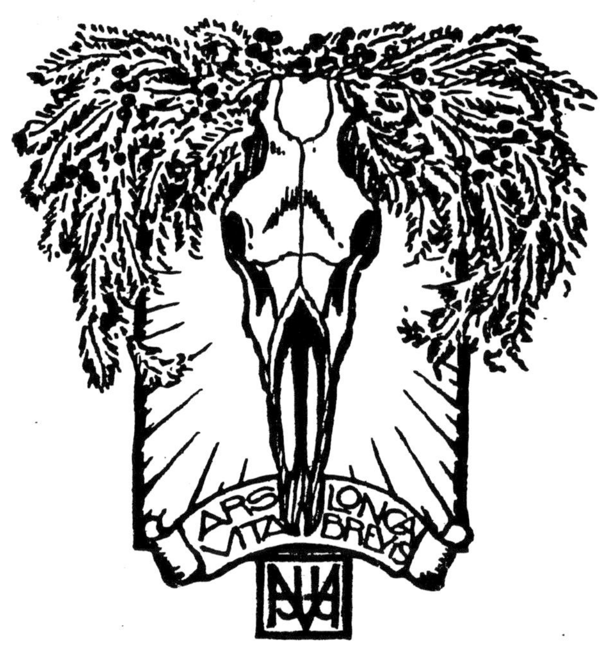

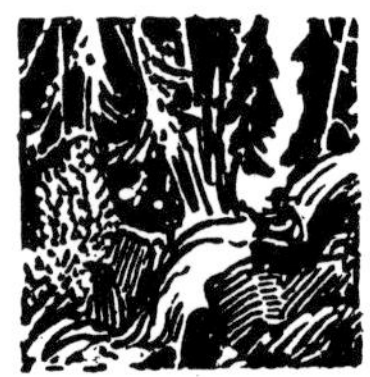

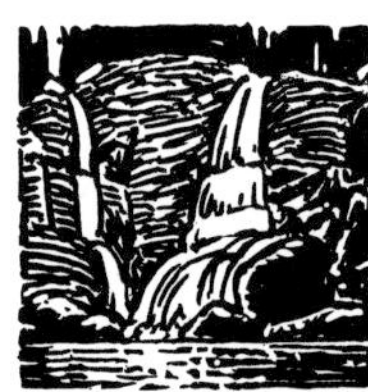

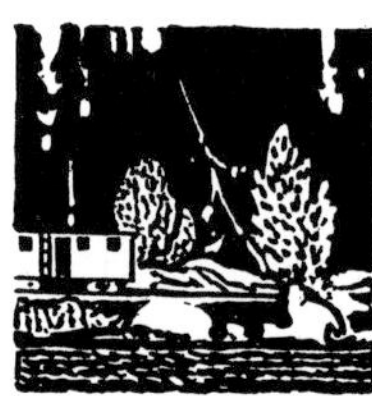

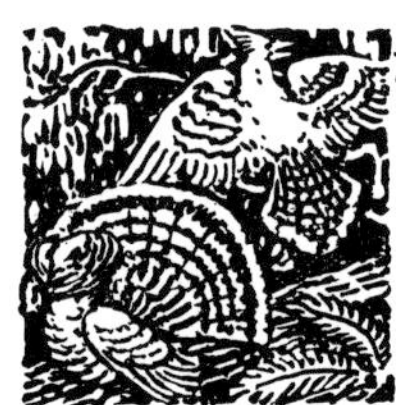

Top: MacDonald designed this image of a moose skull topped with evergreen and red berries and below, a monogram formed from the artists' initials, which was painted on A.C.R. 10557
Bottom: J.E.H. MacDonald, "Ars Longa, Vita Brevis," 1919
The Lamps *(December 1919), pages 33, 34, 36, 38, 39*

tops or rock and maple calls for sketching. The canoeists are off down the river on a similar quest, gliding through the yellow floating leaves, and breaking the still reflections of crimson and gold and green with waving streamers of sky color, until they land where the silent Agawa wakes in a long rapid."[10]

The imagination of these artists made them into explorers. Algoma, they felt, was the preserve of only a few people – the railroad men, a few woodsmen, and themselves. Like discoverers of old, they named lakes, many of them not on the map. As Jackson wrote later: "The bright sparkling lakes we named after people we admired like Thomson and MacCallum; to the swampy ones, all messed up with moose tracks, we gave the names of critics who disparaged us."[11]

MacDonald was the person who most appreciated the concrete reality of what he had seen in Algoma. Paintings such as his *The Wild River* echo many of the words in his first letter – the rocks look huge and powerful, although the "snaky"-shaped river is foamy, not quiet. *Falls, Montreal River* also reveals MacDonald's thoughts. In the painting we see the winding canyon, the curving river, and fine trees – all painted convincingly but in a dynamic way with hot coloration and bold brushstrokes. In yet a third painting, *Algoma Waterfall*, MacDonald studied the subject of waterfalls from the bottom of a hillside, stressing the height of the falling water. The effect in all three paintings is somehow mutable, as though the water emerges from a space near, behind, or even in front of the viewer and dissolves somewhere in the distance or the foreground.

But Harris used Algoma as a source of imagery to distill his thoughts of spiritual life in visual terms. In them, Harris called on all his resources – lessons from Post-Impressionist masters, such as Vincent van Gogh with his imperious handling and Paul Gauguin with his coral-and-mango-coloured visions, to transform turbulent cascades into powerful design, paring his imagery into powerful shape.

In 1921, Harris and Jackson discovered the north shore of Lake Superior and Harris quickly realized he had found what for him was the perfect painting country. (He would visit it again in the autumns of 1924 and 1927.) In 1922, he discovered Coldwell and nearby Pic Island, about half the journey west along the north shore from Sault Ste. Marie to Thunder Bay, which also became favourite painting places. Lake Superior fulfilled his desires for a simplified, pared-down land, with an effect of grandeur. The water seemed to stretch to infinity.

At the time he painted *Above Lake Superior*, one of his most important paintings, Harris was becoming increasingly involved with a semi-spiritual movement called theosophy. The painting marks a turn away from his earlier work, which he called the decorative phase, to a new phase that would lead, in increasing steps, to abstraction. To understand this development we must understand Harris, the man and the artist.

Lawren Stewart Harris was born in 1885 in Brantford, Ontario, about a hundred kilometres southwest of Toronto. As a youngster, he suffered from medical problems and had to spend much of his time in bed or confined to the house. His troubles stemmed from the circumstances of his birth and occurred, according to family legend, because he was stillborn – or what looked like it for a short time. The few minutes' delay of breath was thought to be responsible for his poor health in childhood and the heart condition that affected him, on and off, throughout his life.

To have imperfect health meant something of a character fault for this high achiever, one he sought to alleviate through activity (and he was very energetic). From the beginning, his thoughts of achievement centred on art. His parents had introduced him to art early, bringing him drawing materials and watercolours as a young child to alleviate his boredom and restlessness. He soon found that his expression was keenly at odds with his physical being: he drew what he could see from his window, the objects in his room, illustrations of stories and family and friends – but he let his imagination run free.

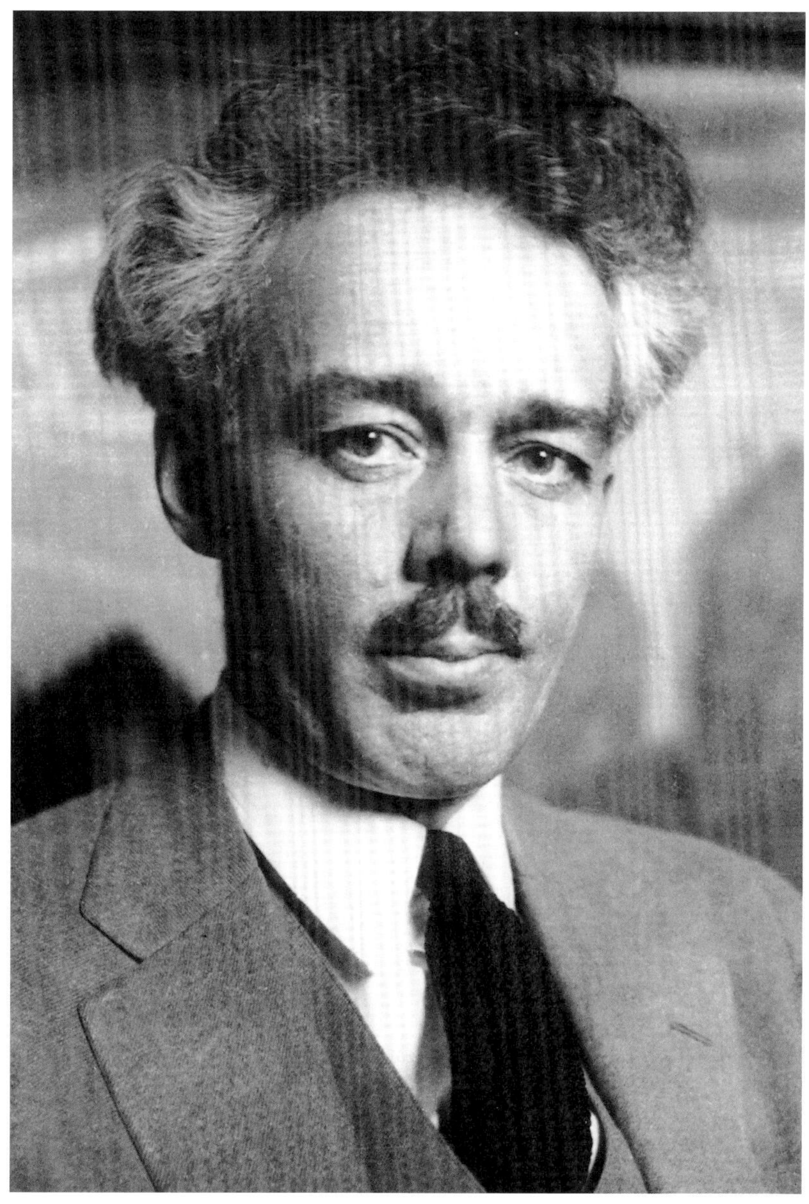

Lawren Harris: Head and shoulders photo portrait of the artist
Photo taken from a lantern slide in the Audio/Visual Library, Art Gallery of Ontario, Toronto
PH-31

Later in life, and especially after a family move to Toronto in 1894, his health improved. He attended school, then University of Toronto, only to follow his natural bent towards art and to sail for Germany in 1904 to study in the cosmopolitan city of Berlin. Here, with teachers such as Franz Skarbina, Fritz von Wille, and Adolf Schlabitz, he learned the basics, painting in the afternoons out of doors, and working in oils during his last two years. In Toronto, where he returned in 1908, he discovered a new quickening of cultural life that centred on the Arts & Letters Club, of which he was one of the founders. In November 1911 at MacDonald's one-person exhibition at the club, Harris met MacDonald for the first time, and the two became good friends. They soon began to travel together on painting expeditions: in the spring of 1912 to Burk's Falls and the Magnetawan River, and then to Mattawa (where Harris photographed MacDonald sketching) and to Temiskaming.

Harris and MacDonald's friendship continued to grow. In January 1913, they travelled to Buffalo together to view a show of "Contemporary Scandinavian Art" at the Albright Art Gallery (today the Albright-Knox Gallery): the show gave them ideas about what they could do for the art of their own country. Both of them noted the decorative treatment used by the Scandinavian artists – the way colour and drawing were transformed into design. Harris and MacDonald not only shared the experience of visiting the show but also an enthusiasm to express its influence through imagery that embodied a direct experience of the Great North, and that would convey the Canadian spirit. Later that year, Harris travelled with MacDonald to the Magnetawan River near Burk's Falls, where MacDonald began to celebrate the waters of northern Canada in paintings such as *A Rapid in the North*, a focused study of cascading water and rocks (see page 91). The waters of Algoma would have meant a renewed challenge to both Harris and MacDonald to paint what was authentically Canadian.

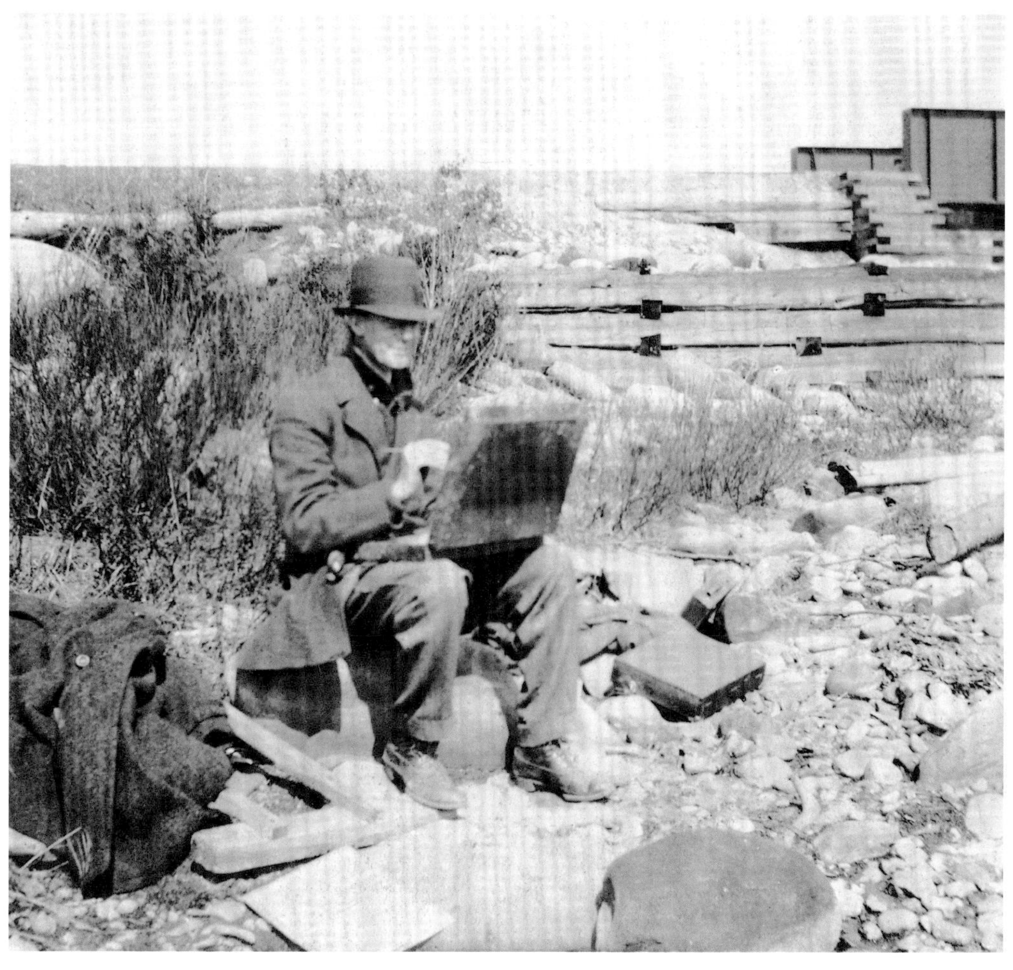

Lawren Harris, photograph of J.E.H. MacDonald painting in Mattawa, April 1913
Thoreau MacDonald collection, courtesy of a private collector

Through these years, however, and particularly in the early 1920s, Harris was changing. Besides meeting MacDonald and many of what became the Group of Seven, as well as Tom Thomson, at the Arts & Letters Club, Harris met Roy Mitchell, a progressive member who promoted experimental ideas in drama. Mitchell introduced Harris to Plato and esoteric Eastern texts.

Mitchell was a member of the Toronto Theosophical Society, a group that later became vitally important to Harris. Theosophy is a synthesis of religions tied to Eastern beliefs that deal with ethics, art and aesthetics, and moral codes. Harris had fallen under the spell of the nineteenth-century Anglo-Russian author Helena Petrova Blavatsky, co-founder in 1875 of the growing international Theosophical Society and the writer of books that plagiarized esoteric texts.

Blavatsky suggested that theosophy is the primordial wisdom-religion, the secret doctrine that underlies all existing religions and scriptures. Harris deeply believed in theosophy: in March 1924, he formally joined the Toronto Theosophical Society. Because of his deeply held beliefs, he wrote for *The Canadian Theosophist*, read papers at conventions, gave radio talks on the subject of theosophy and tried, not too successfully, to convert his friends. In contrast to the confining Presbyterian and Baptist obsessions with individual sin and damnation with which he had been raised, theosophy subscribed to no creed or dogma. It offered the individual a way to rise above ordinary laws and moral codes. For Harris, this meant greater freedom. In terms of his art, it meant new subjects and a new way of treating them.

Harris, who had developed a mystical vision of nature from reading philosophers and mystics, therefore began to convey a more austere, intellectual quality in painting an outdoors scene, one involved with light, which he used to convey the essence. This vision began to be apparent in his paintings of the landscape around Lake Superior, in which he combined the natural and the spiritual. For instance, in Harris's painting *North Shore,*

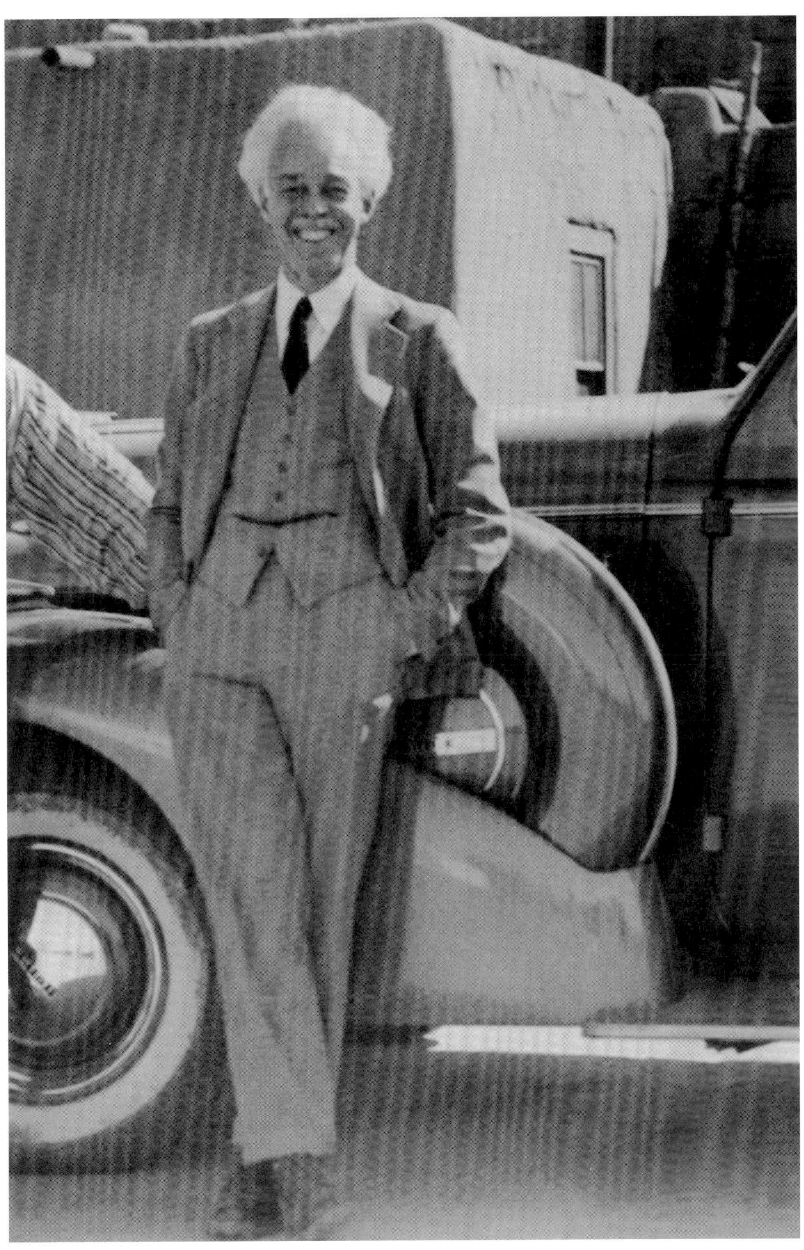

Unknown photographer, Lawren Harris in Santa Fe, New Mexico, c. 1939
Photograph courtesy Art Gallery of Ontario, Toronto

Lake Superior of a stump set high on a rocky shore above Lake Superior, he painted a bank of clouds in the distance that encircles a flow of illumination from an unseen source (see page 59). Jackson later recalled that the stump was almost lost in the bush, nowhere within sight of the lake, but Harris isolated it and gave it a nobler background. In his later paintings of Lake Superior, Harris's forms became increasingly abstract. He continually strove to express, ever more intensely, a spiritual and mystical quality.

Another great subject for Harris was the Canadian Rockies, which he visited every summer between 1924 and 1928. In 1924, he painted the waters of Maligne Lake, Jasper Park (see page 53). In the scene, he captured an extraordinary sense of stillness, reinforced by a colour range of greys, greens, and blues and the painting's careful compositional balance. A later work, *Isolation Peak* (the title is imaginary since there is no such mountain), carries the story one step further, with its explicit contours, floodlit pyramid-shaped peak, and sense of quiet (see page 61). Paintings of icebergs, which he developed after a trip to the Arctic in 1930, allowed him to select even more enigmatic forms. Such paintings, by demonstrating Harris's interest in the spirit of the scene rather than its literal representation, reveal that Harris had started down the road to abstraction. In 1934, he became an abstract artist. Abstraction for him was full of alluring possibilities; and he enjoyed the lack of conventional direction to his work. Even as an abstract artist, in some of his works, he sought to indicate the waters in a way that expressed his emotional attachment, often by a simple wave rhythm as in *Abstract Sketch* (see page 65).

His experiences in the Canadian North and particularly his conception of the waters in Algoma, along with those of MacDonald, Jackson, and Johnston, started the flow of powerful images of rivers in the sourcebook of the Group of Seven. For all these men, the scenes meant a definite marking-off of the subject, one they never forgot. Later, they continued to create paintings based on these mental images.

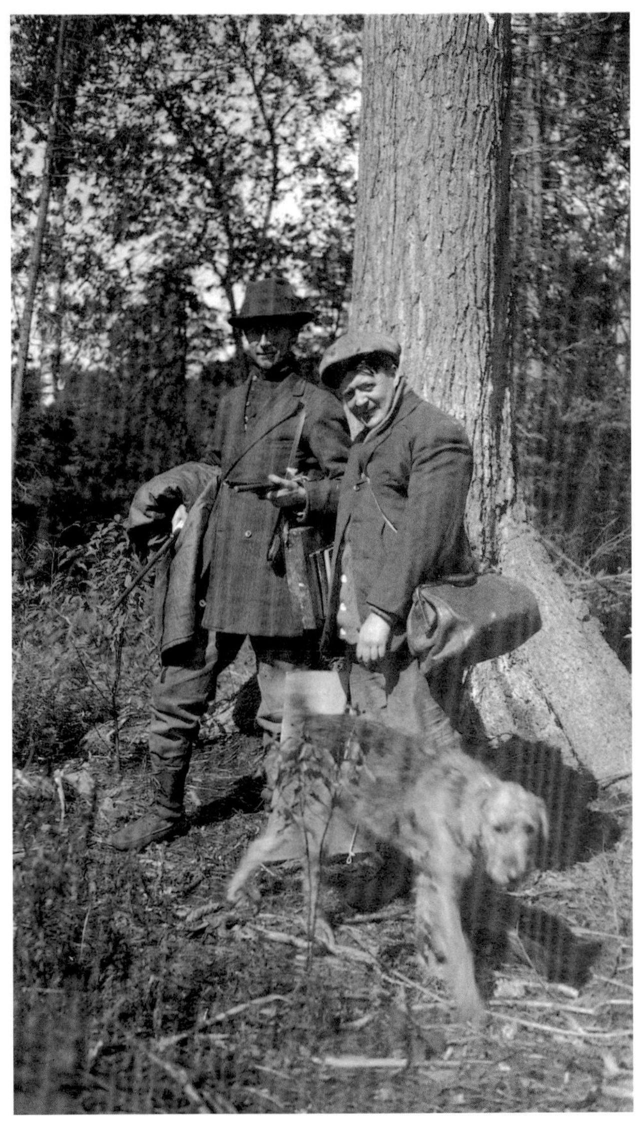

J.E.H. MacDonald, Frank H. Johnston, and "Woofie" in Algoma
Photograph 1/9, Thoreau MacDonald collection,
courtesy of a private collector

For artists such as Harris, MacDonald, and Johnston, Algoma was a high point in their work, a moment when they were seized with elation at the scene and painted the beauties of the place; even Johnston worked with the sort of fury that inspired Harris and MacDonald (see pages 76 to 81). Other artists, such as Tom Thomson, painted waters differently. His scenes, where the water is often parallel to the picture plane and seems to flow close by the observer, evoke an equally intense, but more private vision (see page 115).

Such paintings help us better understand the concept of nature for the Group of Seven and the way it was formed from many sources. Lynda Jessup, historian of Canadian culture, has written perceptively of the way that Group of Seven paintings were tied to Canadian tourism when it emerged as a state-coordinated industry in the 1920s.[12] The Group's image of waters in a wilderness, empty of inhabitants, reflected a romantic notion of nature, a way of looking at the landscape that is characteristic of tourism.

This lavish celebration of a romantic ideal, more characteristic of Ontario regionalism than of the whole country, sounds a melancholy note today when our idea of nationhood has changed so fundamentally. But in its time, the image was compelling. The vision of Lawren Harris, the Group of Seven, and Tom Thomson became central to our idea of Canada. In this vision, the waters of the country linked us all to Canada's past and future. They were the way a generation travelled to its destiny.

Notes

1. Lawren Harris to J.E.H. MacDonald, undated letters of 1918 and 1919 (J.E.H. MacDonald Papers, National Archives of Canada, Ottawa, MG30 (D111)). I am indebted for these observations to the book by Peter Larisey, *Light for a Cold Land* (Toronto: Dundurn Press, 1993), page 34, 185n38.
2. I am indebted here again to Larisey (see above note 1), who cites Lawren Harris, "The Group of Seven in Canadian History," page 34, 186n1.
3. F.B. Housser, *A Canadian Art Movement: The Story of the Group of Seven* (Toronto: Macmillan, 1926), pages 137–38; J.E.H. MacDonald to Joan MacDonald, sometime in September 1918, quoted here from the original letter, courtesy of a private collector (see the Appendix for the full text).
4. MacDonald to Joan MacDonald, sometime in September 1918.
5. A.Y. Jackson to Florence Clement, 29 September [1919], cited in Charles C. Hill, *The Group of Seven: Art for a Nation* (Ottawa and Toronto: National Gallery of Canada and McClelland & Stewart, 1995), page 80.
6. A.Y. Jackson, *A Painter's Country: The Autobiography of A.Y. Jackson* (Toronto: Clarke, Irwin, 1958), pages 56–57.
7. J.E.H. MacDonald, "A.C.R. 10557," *The Lamps* (December 1919), pages 33–39.
8. MacDonald, "A.C.R. 10557," page 34.
9. MacDonald, "A.C.R. 10557," page 34.
10. MacDonald, "A.C.R. 10557," page 35.
11. Jackson, *A Painter's Country*, page 57.
12. See Lynda Jessup, "The Group of Seven and the Tourist Landscape in Western Canada, or the More Things Change ..." *Journal of Canadian Studies* 37 (Spring 2002), pages 144–79.

Chronology

Algoma

1918

May. Lawren Harris and Dr. J.M. MacCallum take the Algoma Central Railway to Stop 123.

10 or 11? September. Harris, MacCallum, MacDonald, and Johnston travel on the Algoma Central Railway in a boxcar, stopping at Canyon.

Sometime in September. MacDonald writes to his wife, Joan MacDonald, from Canyon, comparing the scene to the *Inferno* (1314) by the Italian poet Dante Alighieri (1265–1321). Johnston paints thirty-three sketches.

1919–1920

September. Harris, MacDonald, Jackson, and Johnston make a second boxcar trip.

18 December–19 January. The Art Gallery of Toronto presents “Algoma Sketches and Pictures by J.E.H. MacDonald, ARCA, Lawren Harris, and Frank H. Johnston.” MacDonald’s *The Wild River* is among the works shown. The short text in the pamphlet accompanying the show suggests that the artists painted the large pictures at home after the trip; other paintings were imaginative summaries. The pamphlet mentions that the train made three stops so that the artists could follow the fall colour: at Canyon, Hubert, and Batchawana.

Spring. Harris, Lismer, MacDonald, and Jackson make a boxcar trip to Algoma.

September. Harris, Jackson, and Johnston make a boxcar trip to Algoma. They rent a cottage on Mongoose Lake.

The Waters

This book is a tribute to the ideal of water – to an art form with an imperative drawn from subject matter that is mutable and mercurial. To focus the significance of the theme, I have chosen the paintings of Lawren Harris, one of the greatest artists in Canadian art, who was a leader in the creation of the Group of Seven and many other artists' organizations, as well as being an inspiration to generations of Canadians. Along with Harris's paintings, I have selected examples of the work of the Group of Seven and, although he wasn't a member, I have included oil sketches by Tom Thomson because Harris was his close friend.

Water had a special meaning for Harris. He was an avid swimmer and diver and found these activities healing to the spirit. Yet, as a painter, water was part of a firm structure he developed; it flows endlessly, grounding his islands and mountains, emphasizing loneliness and the coldness of the world.

Curiously, although Harris had been the person who organized the trips that brought friends like J.E.H. MacDonald to discover the tumultuous waters of the North and address them in paint, he found in himself a certain resistance to Algoma, MacDonald's favourite painting location. Like MacDonald, he loved its wild richness and clarity of colour, but as he told A.Y. Jackson, the landscape in Algoma was too opulent for him; he wanted a place that was more bare and stark, the kind of locale he found, along with Jackson, in 1921 in Lake Superior. Here too, he painted water, although often the undulating rhythms seem magically to turn into ice.

Whether turbulent or freezing up, the waters of Canada are part of our heritage; they are part of what makes us Canadian. All Canadians have a stake in their history – as the federal, provincial, and territorial governments realize. In 1984, they established the Canadian Heritage Rivers System to conserve and protect the best examples of our river heritage and give them nationwide recognition. Today, this cooperative program provides stewardship for thirty-nine rivers, with more on the waiting list. May these splendid, free-flowing rivers always be preserved by the dedicated people who care for them.

List of Plates

(Where a title is duplicated, the collection is given.)

Water

Franklin Carmichael, 1890–1945

St. Antoine, 1924

Carmichael was one of the few artists of the Group of Seven to paint a waterfall face on, as if he were standing in the waters at the bottom. This was a difficult task, but one that he handles concisely, using a medium that he found congenial, watercolour, with delicacy and vigour.

Franklin Carmichael
Watercolour over conté, 22 x 26.8 cm
McMichael Canadian Art Collection, Kleinburg (1968.25.3)

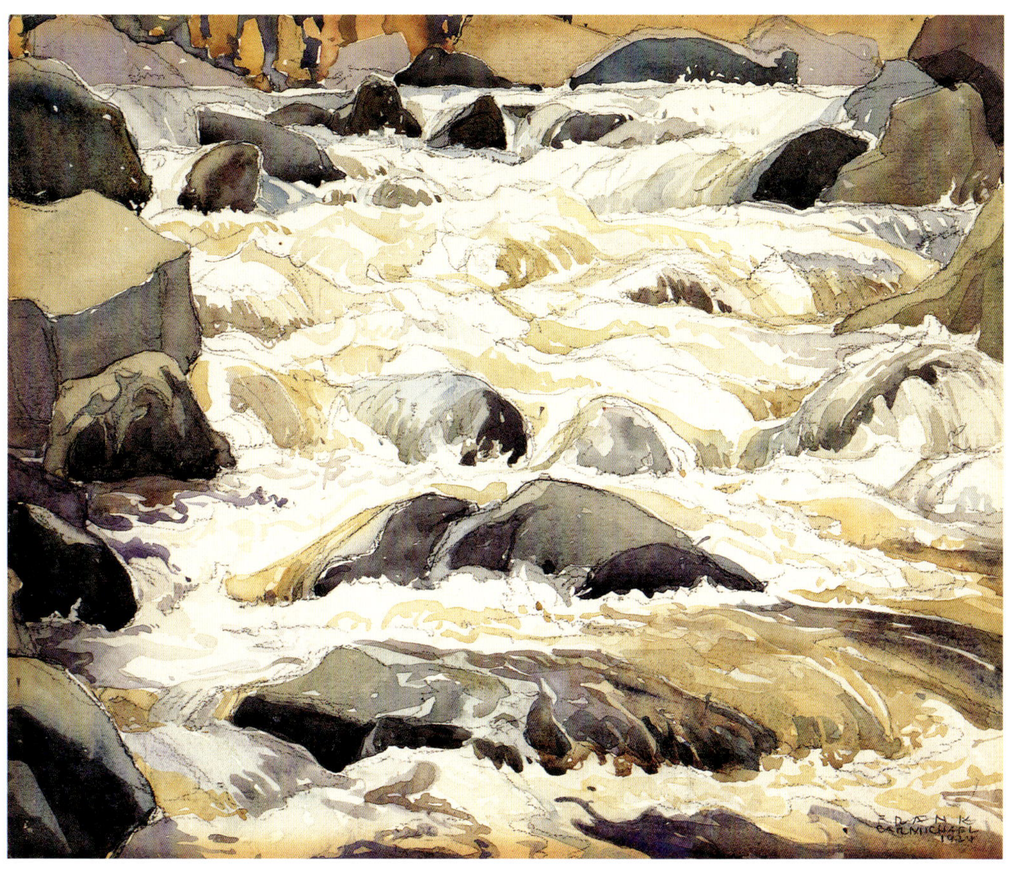
FRANK
CARMICHAEL

Buck's Slide near Carnarvon, 1940

Carmichael painted this image of rapids in a way characteristic of the Group of Seven, creating a strong diagonal that almost runs corner to corner of the painting. Once again, he seems to be standing in the midst of the waters to record the view.

Franklin Carmichael

Oil on plywood, 30.1 x 40.7 cm

McMichael Canadian Art Collection, Kleinburg (1979.25.1)

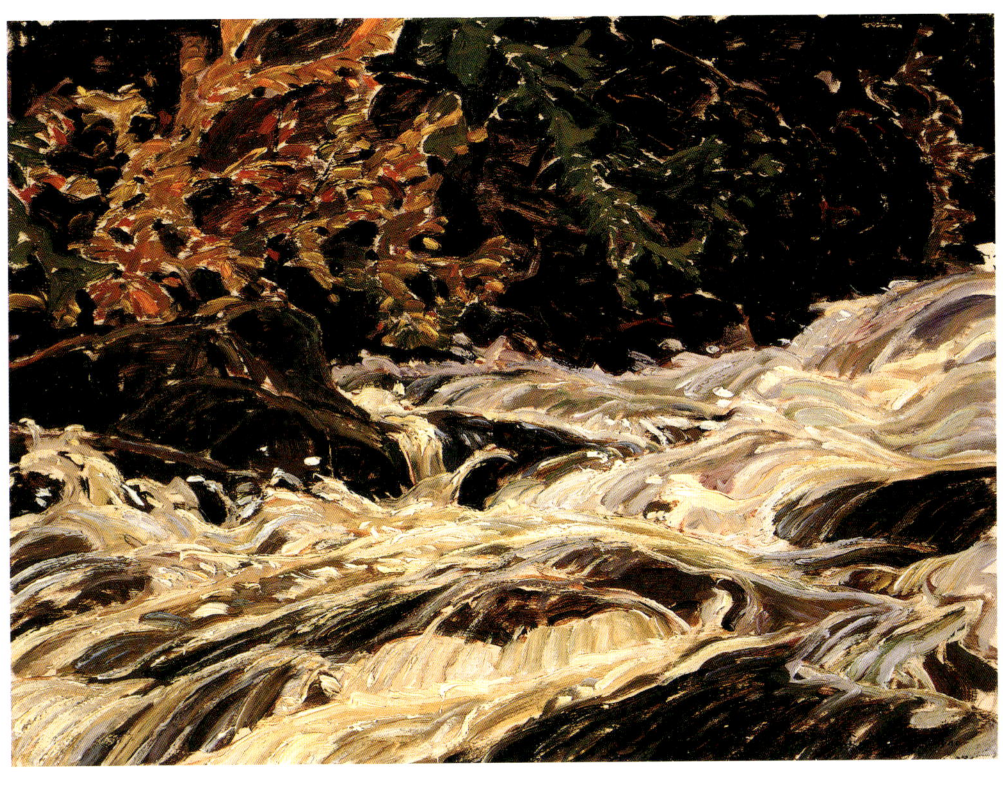

A.J. Casson, 1898–1992

Magnetawan River near Canal Rapids, 1934

In the history of the Group of Seven, A.J. Casson seems to exist on the quiet fringes. But in the context of art between the two World Wars, he's an important figure, and this painting gives more than a hint of the reason why. It is a distinctive powerful vision on the theme of waters, painted directly and with strength.

On the back of the work the artist wrote "painted on a camping trip with J.S. Hallam." Hallam (1899–1953) was one of Casson's painting peers.

Oil on board, 28.3 x 28.8 cm

Tom Thomson Memorial Art Gallery, Owen Sound (977.008)

Gift of the artist on the occasion of the gallery's 10th anniversary

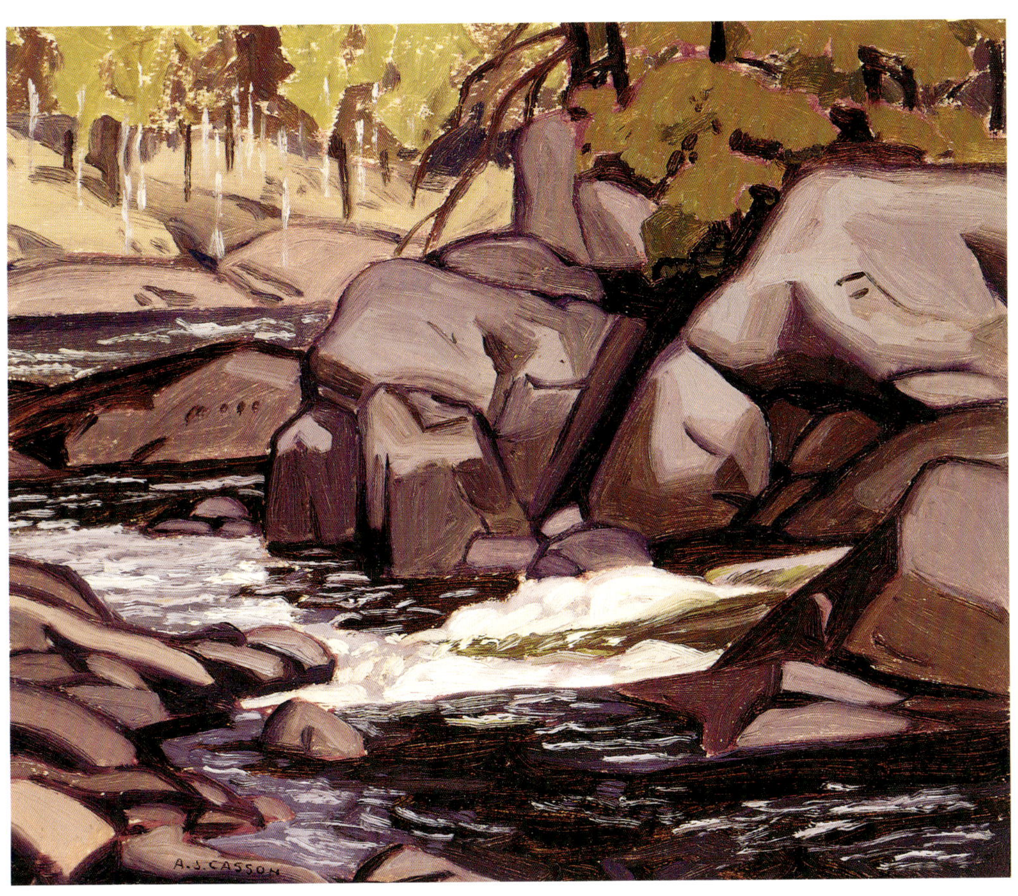
A.J. CASSON

Falls on the Little Mississippi River

The waterfalls are in the back- and middle ground. In the foreground are quieter waters on which float lilypads. The Little Mississippi River is in Ontario in Renfrew County.

Oil on panel, 30.4 x 38.0 cm
McMichael Canadian Art Collection, Kleinburg (1995.7.3)
Donated by Dr. and Mrs. Heaslip

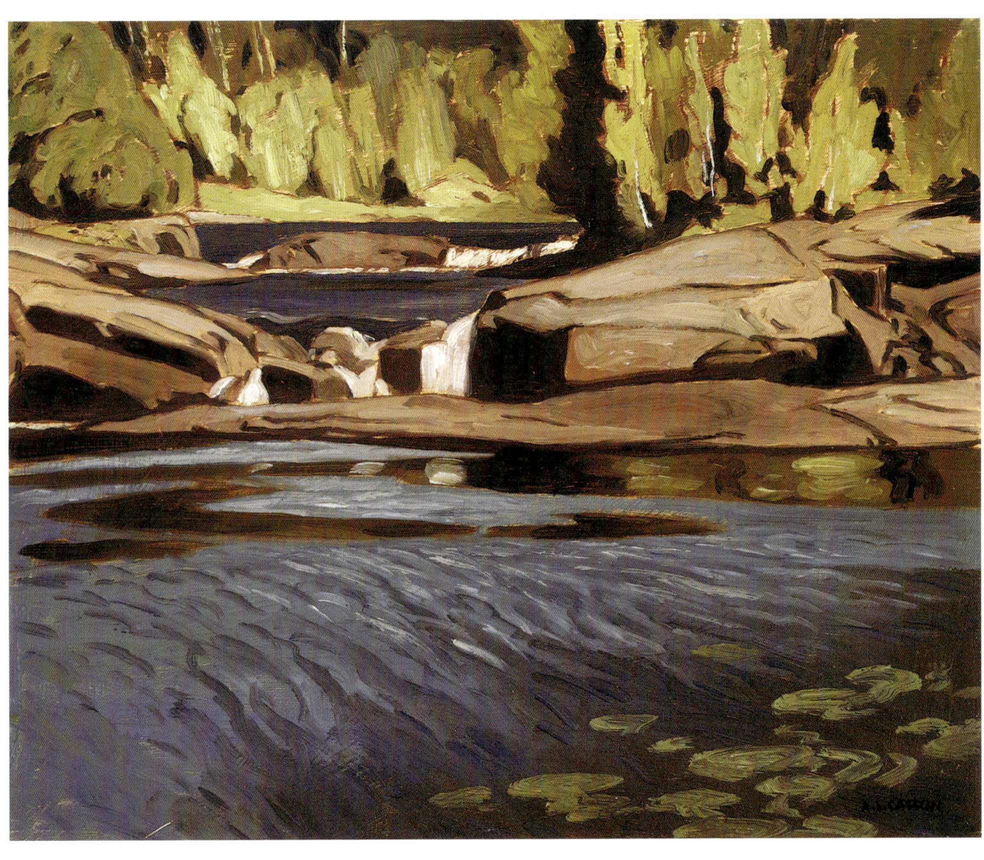

Lionel LeMoine FitzGerald, 1890–1956

Assiniboine River from Maryland Bridge, 1918

FitzGerald painted the Assiniboine River in Winnipeg with bold clarity, combining the different blues and purples of the water and contrasting them with white snow, pink banks, and the forms of white, blue, and red-orange distant houses and dilapidated barns. For him, water provided an unrivalled chance at a colour feast.

L.L. FitzGerald
Oil on canvas, 44.8 x 60.0 cm
Agnes Etherington Art Centre, Queen's University, Kingston (13-054)
Gift from the Douglas M. Duncan Collection, 1970

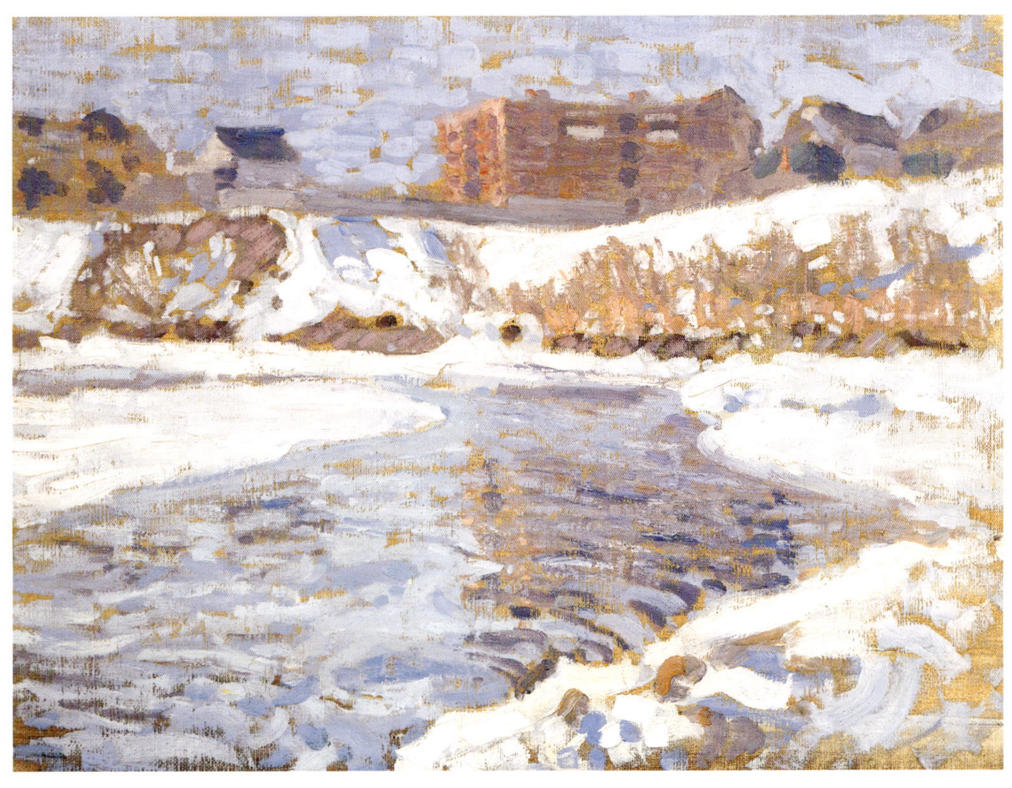

Untitled, River, n.d.

FitzGerald had enough ideas for three or four different careers. His detailed, low-toned studies of landscape and still life include paintings in which he used imagery drawn from Winnipeg, where he lived. This animated drawing in pastel of a river in Winnipeg, likely the Assiniboine at nightfall, has a magical effect.

L.L. FitzGerald
Chalk pastel on paper, 28.2 x 37.2 cm
The Winnipeg Art Gallery (G-70-130)
Gift from the Douglas M. Duncan Collection

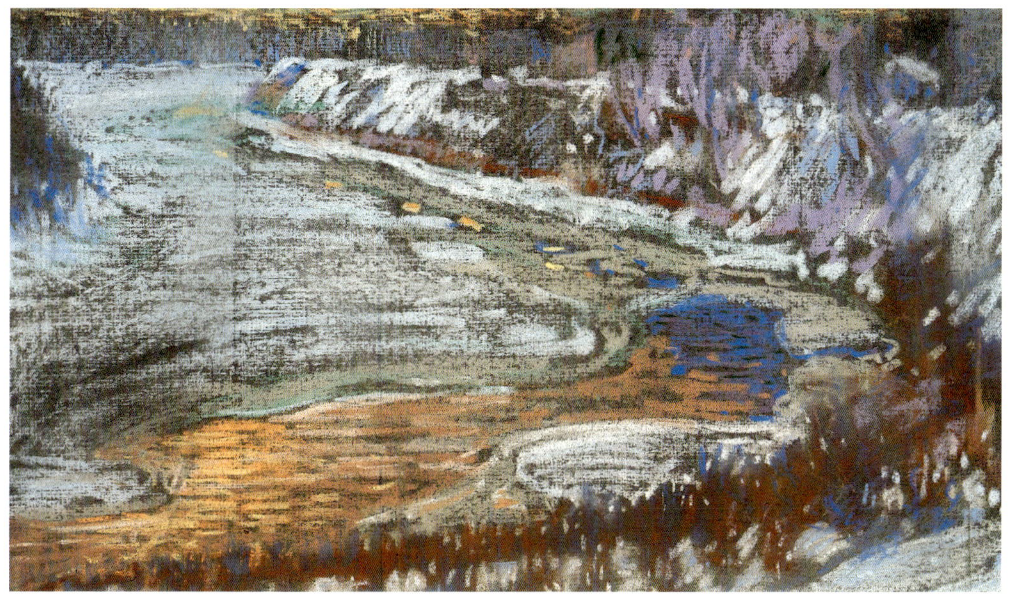

Lawren Harris, 1885–1970

Agawa Waterfall, 1919

When he was in Algoma, Harris liked to paint the waterfalls; sometimes he sang, with the rushing water as an accompaniment, wrote J.E.H. MacDonald. This sprightly sketch shows his delight in the landscape he found in Algoma, with its many ravines and canyons through which ran rivers, streams, and springs, bolstered by huge granite rocks and hardwood, spruce, and pine.

Lawren Harris
Oil on board, 26.7 x 34.3 cm
The Thomson Collection (PC-353)

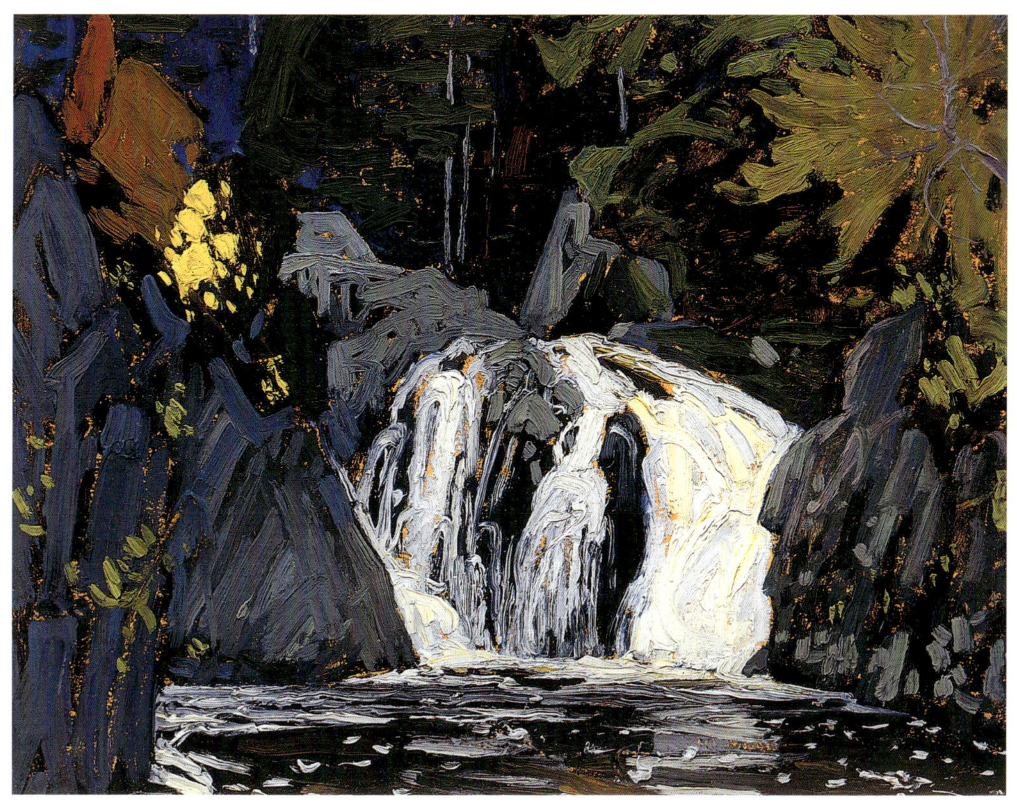

Waterfall, Algoma Canyon, 1919

Harris used this small but powerful painting of the Agawa River towards a larger painting, today in the Art Gallery of Hamilton, which he showed in the 1920 Group of Seven exhibition "Waterfall, Algoma." In the sketch, he stressed the limpid flow of water – in the finished painting, the rocky canyon wall. The development from sketch to canvas suggests that while Harris responded intuitively to form and movement, he startlingly revised his view later, preferring to construct crisper, tougher, more finished and monumental shapes.

Lawren Harris

Oil on board, 26.x 40 cm

The Thomson Collection (PC-979)

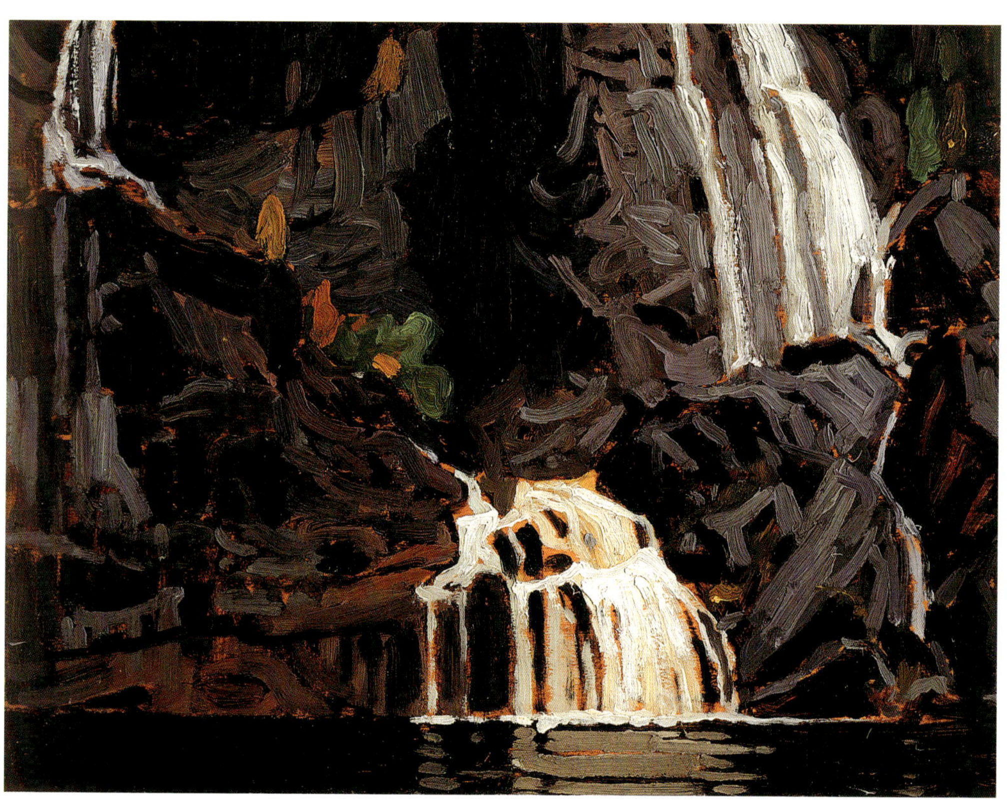

Waterfall, Algoma, c. 1920

Harris called Algoma a veritable paradise; he loved the clarity of form and colour he found there. In this painting, based on several of the sketches he made in Algoma, he emphasized the interlocking shapes of the rocks and the vertical falls of water. In a 1920 *Canadian Courier* article titled "Are These New Canadian Painters Crazy?" critic Augustus Bridle described the picture as a "sullen and powerful epic," which hardly suggests its colour and lyricism. Harris selected the painting to be shown in the 1920 Group of Seven exhibition, thus emphasizing its importance to him.

Lawren Harris
Oil on canvas, 120.0 x 139.7 cm
Art Gallery of Hamilton
Gift of the Women's Committee, 1957

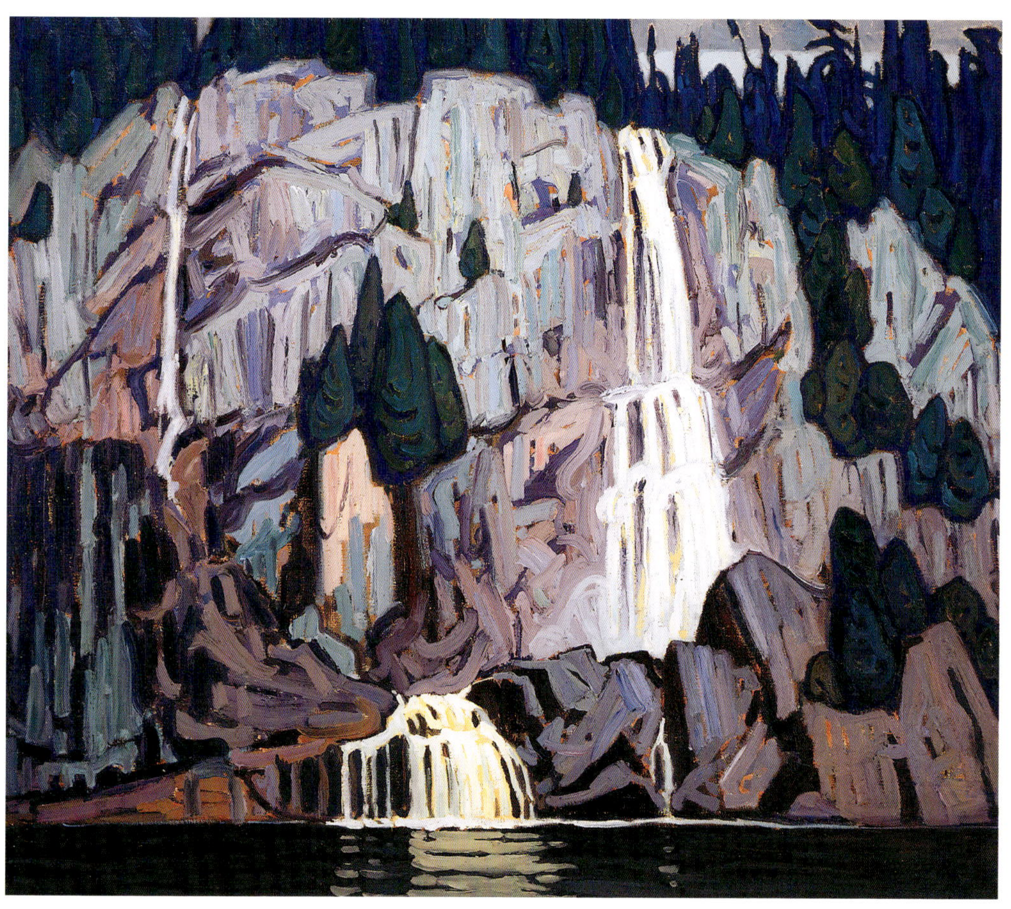

Montreal River, 1920

Harris painted this beautiful small oil on one of his Algoma trips. Here he glimpsed the Montreal River from a height, between trees. Notice the way in which the water changes colour from a dark foreground to a lighter distance because of a stray beam of light finding its way through a break in the clouds.

Lawren Harris
Oil on board, 27.0 x 34.7 cm
McMichael Canadian Art Collection, Kleinburg (1966.16.77)
Gift of the Founders, Robert and Signe McMichael

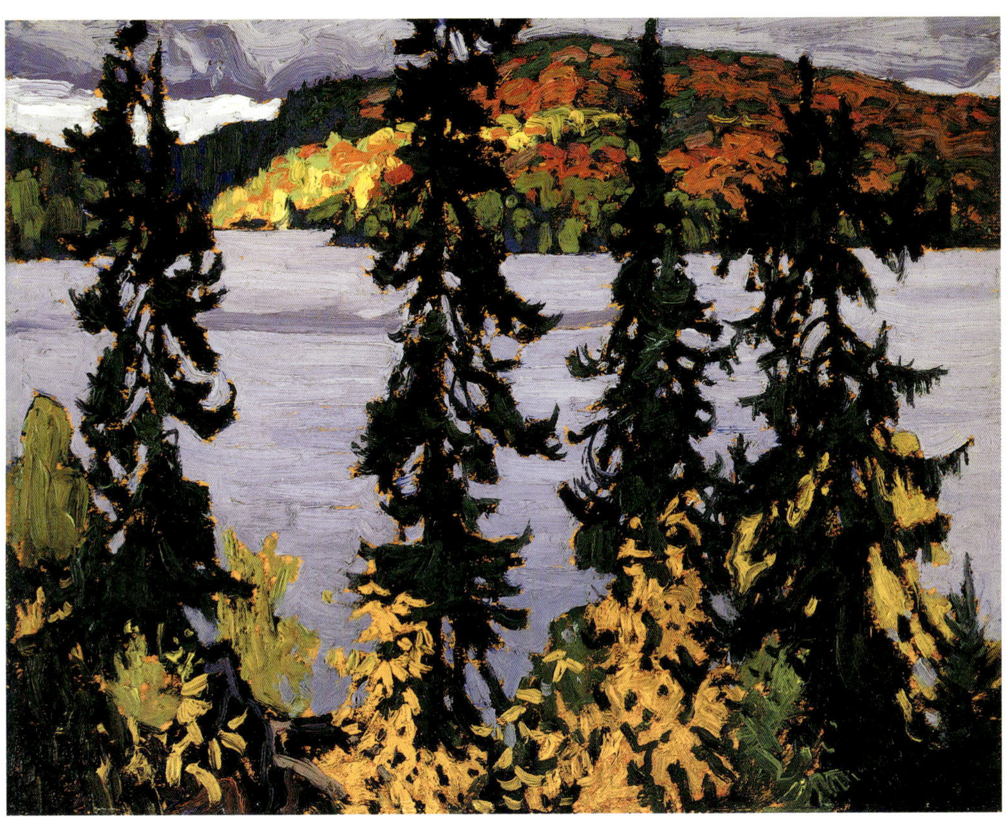

Spring on the Oxtongue River, 1924

In developing the sketch for this painting into a canvas, Harris evolved a rigorously formal and expansively illusory mode of expression. This spare, almost austere, painting reverberates with Harris's thoughts about painting: as craft, philosophy, and lifelong pursuit.

Lawren Harris
Oil on canvas, 82.2 x 102.2 cm
Gallery Lambton, Sarnia (956.001.001)
Industries Art Fund purchase, 1956

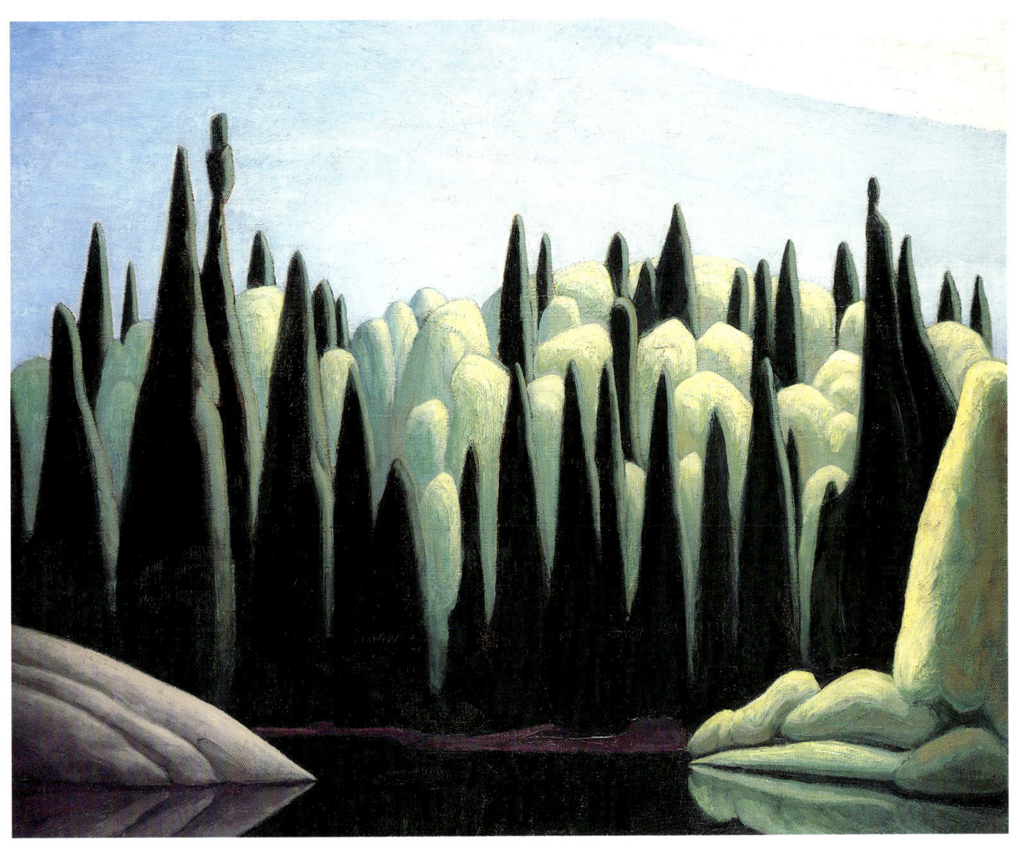

Malinge Lake, Jasper Park, 1924

Harris captures in this scene a sense of stillness, reinforced by a colour range of grey, blue, and green and the painting's careful compositional balance.

Lawren Harris
Oil on canvas, 122.8 x 152.8 cm
National Gallery of Canada, Ottawa (3541)
Purchased, 1928

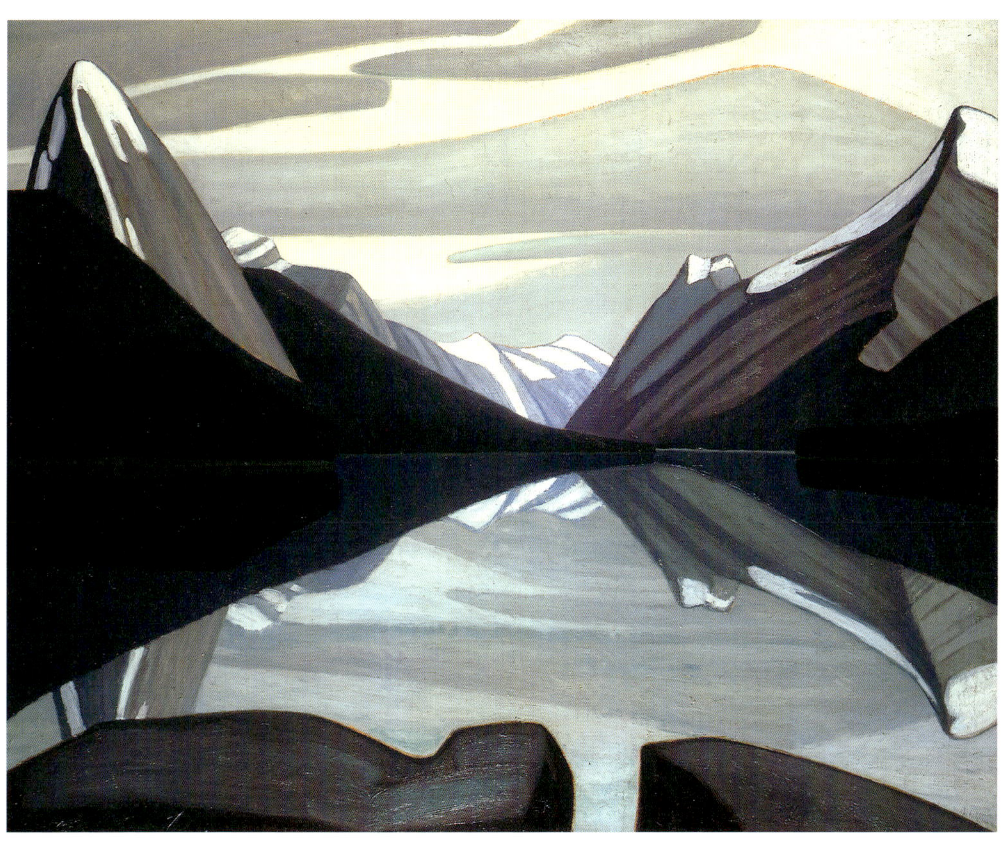

Pic Island, c. 1924

In 1922, Harris discovered the town of Coldwell and nearby Pic Island, about half the journey west along the north shore from Sault Ste. Marie to Thunder Bay, which became one of his favourite painting places. Lake Superior fulfilled his desire for a pared-down land with an effect of grandeur and even of organic life. *Pic Island* almost looks like an animal crouched on the surface of the water.

Lawren Harris
Oil on canvas, 123.3 x 153.9 cm
McMichael Canadian Art Collection, Kleinburg (1968.7.4)
Gift of Col. R.S. McLaughlin

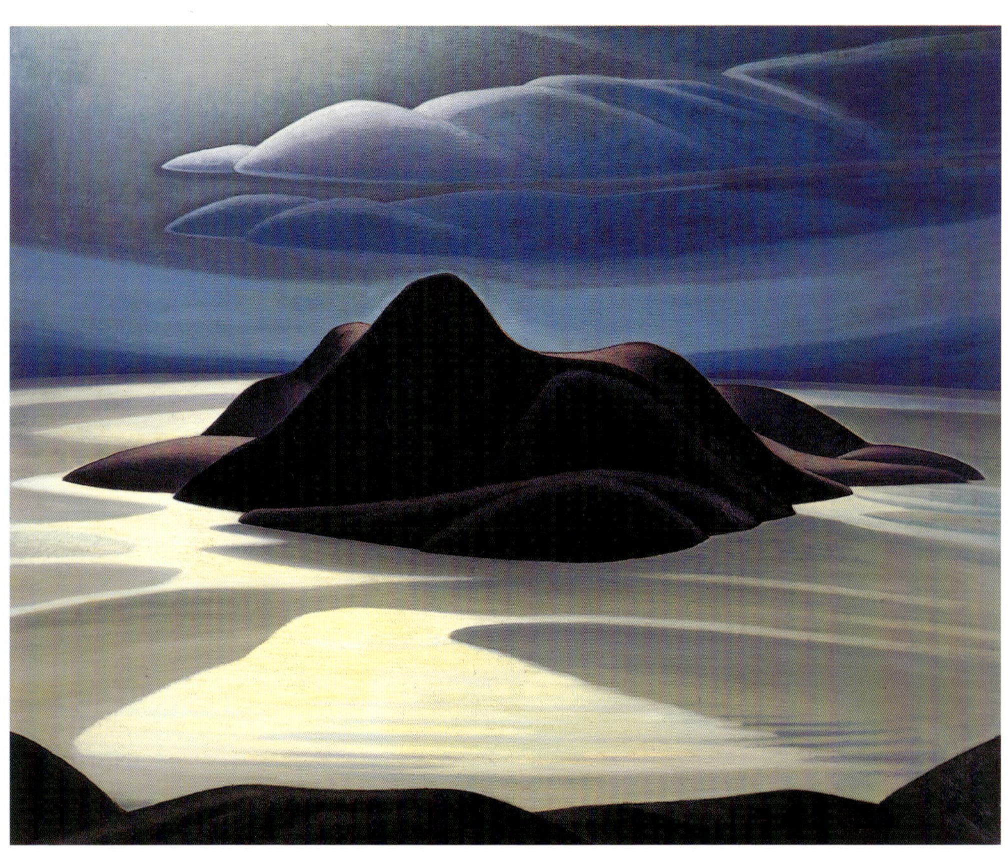

Algoma Waterfall, c. 1926

The austere, intellectual quality of Harris's thought is expressed in his work, in which he used a restricted palette, smooth brushwork, and a sparse type of composition. He simplified nature to its lucid fundamental forms. Using a sketch he had made on-site (see page 43), he stressed the essential shapes of the scene – making an area of the background around a rocky shape more mysterious and freezing up the effect of the flowing water so that it balances on the borderline of the abstract. In this great canvas, the image of water looks suggestive, almost as if it were a metaphor for something else, purity perhaps.

Lawren Harris

Oil on canvas, 87.6 x 102.9 cm

Imperial Oil Limited Collection, Toronto

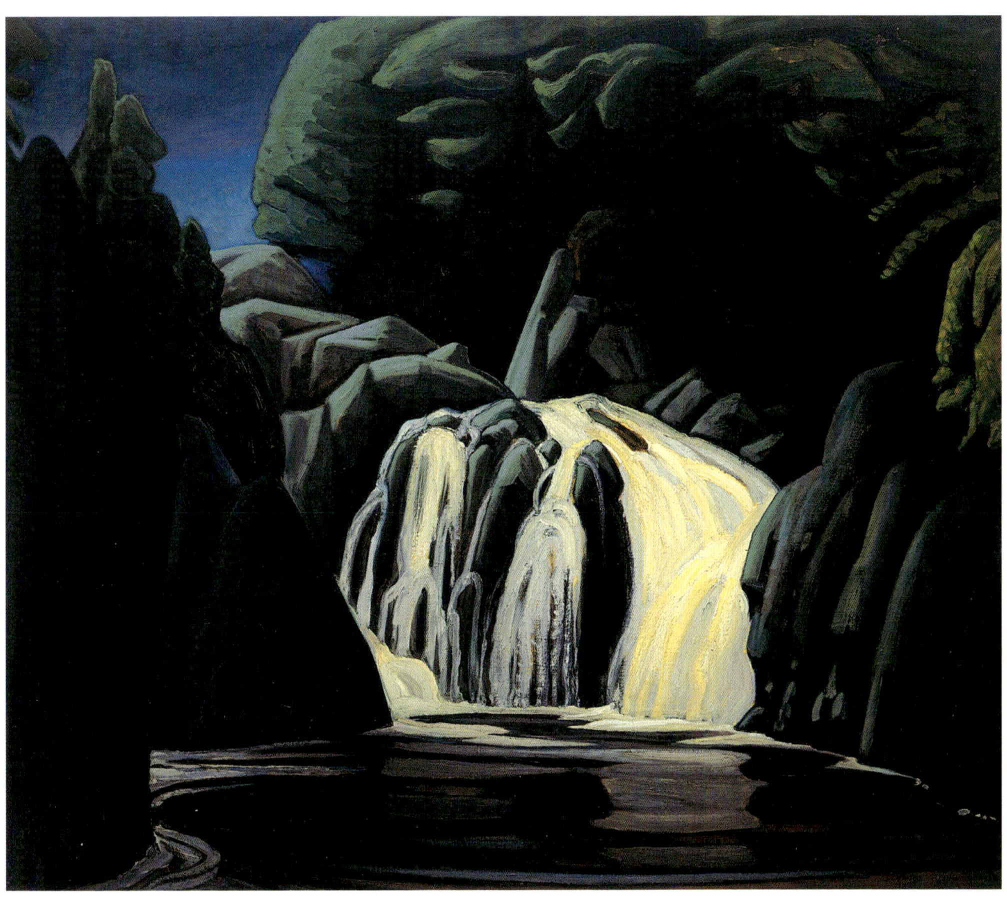

North Shore, Lake Superior, 1926

Some critics consider this painting the most important of Harris's work. Harris discovered the image on a trip to the Coldwell area with A.Y. Jackson in 1925. The stump was almost lost in the bush, Jackson wrote later, but Harris isolated it and placed it against the background of the lake to express more intensely a spiritual and mystical quality.

Lawren Harris

Oil on canvas, 101.2 x 128.3 cm

National Gallery of Canada, Ottawa (3708)

Purchased 1930

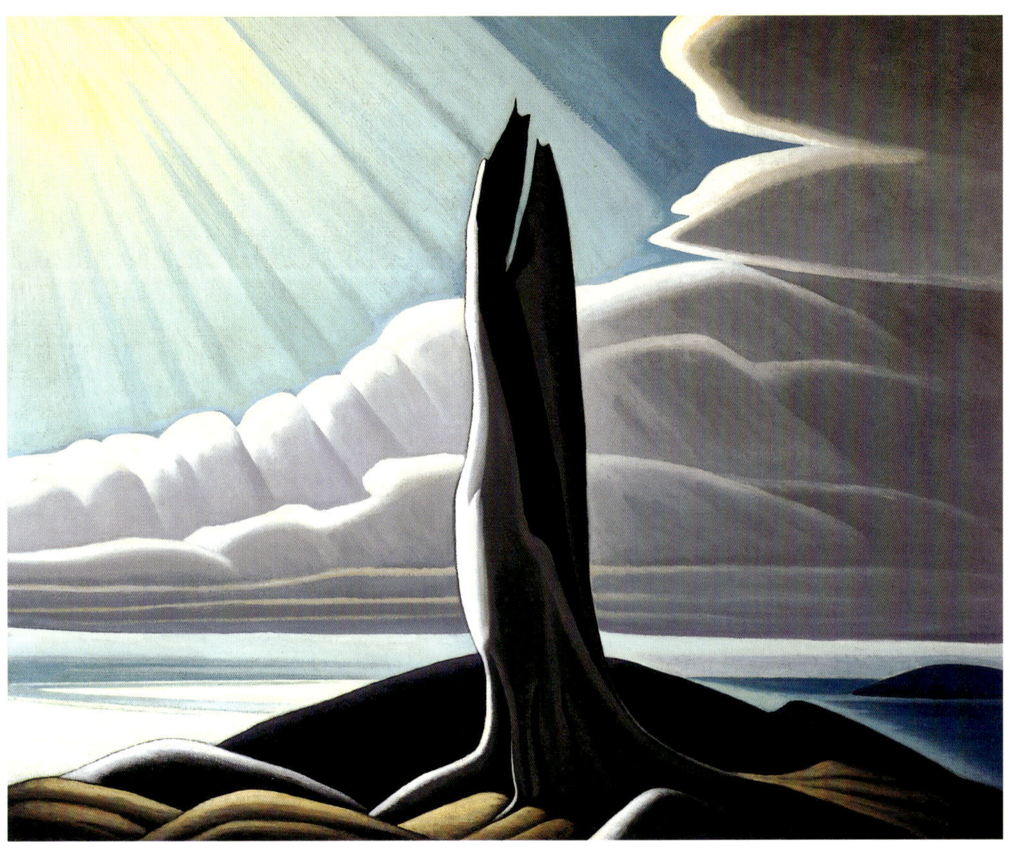

Isolation Peak, c. 1930

One of Harris's great subjects in the 1920s was the Canadian Rockies, which he visited every summer between 1924 and 1928. He composed this painting from his imagination and memories of his trips – there is no such mountain. The image reveals the power, majesty, and silence of these Western spaces. For Harris, the peak was a majestic embodiment of transcendental thought. The painting builds up to an almost supernatural shape.

Lawren Harris

Oil on canvas, 104.2 x 124.5 cm

Hart House Permanent Collection, University of Toronto (46.1)

Purchased with income from the Harold and Murray Wrong Memorial Fund, 1946

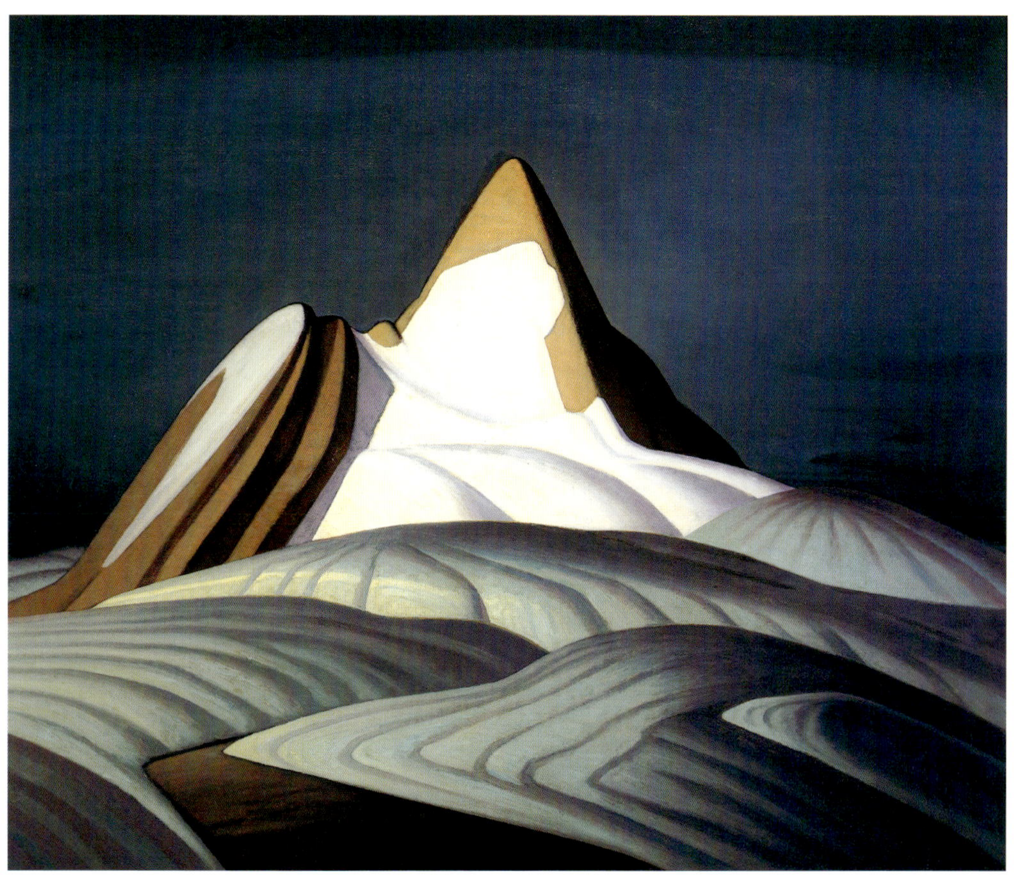

Icebergs, Davis Strait, 1930

In other works, developed from trips to the Arctic in 1930, Harris selected icebergs and ice floes with which to create images of tranquility and to transcend the ephemeral in nature. Their appeal lies in the architecture of nature, its eloquent calm, and the way in which such forms express spiritual values.

Lawren Harris

Oil on canvas, 121.9 x 152.4 cm

McMichael Canadian Art Collection, Kleinburg

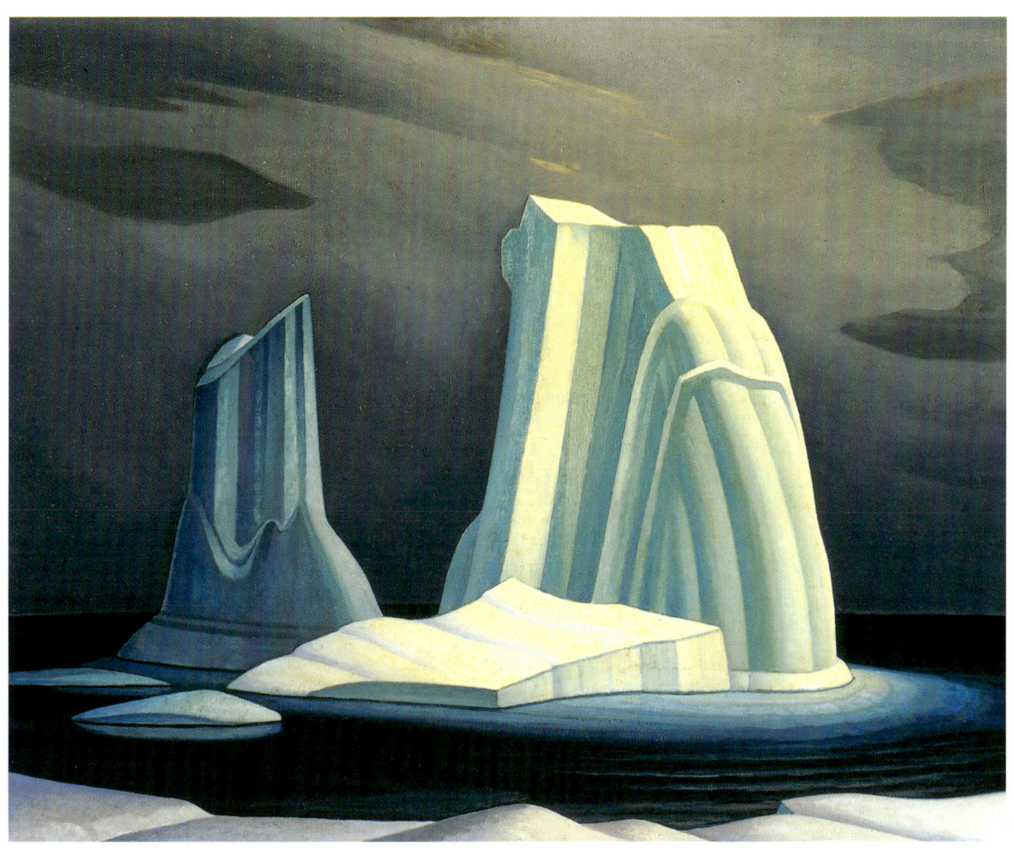

Abstract Sketch, c. 1937

Even after he became an abstract artist in 1934, Harris continued to evoke waters. Note the ghostly waters seen from below in this abstract sketch. This sketch by Lawren Harris was a gift to painter Jock Macdonald when Macdonald moved from Vancouver to Calgary.

Lawren Harris
Oil on wood panel
30.7 x 38.0 cm
McMichael Canadian Art Collection, Kleinburg
Purchase 1971
1971.8

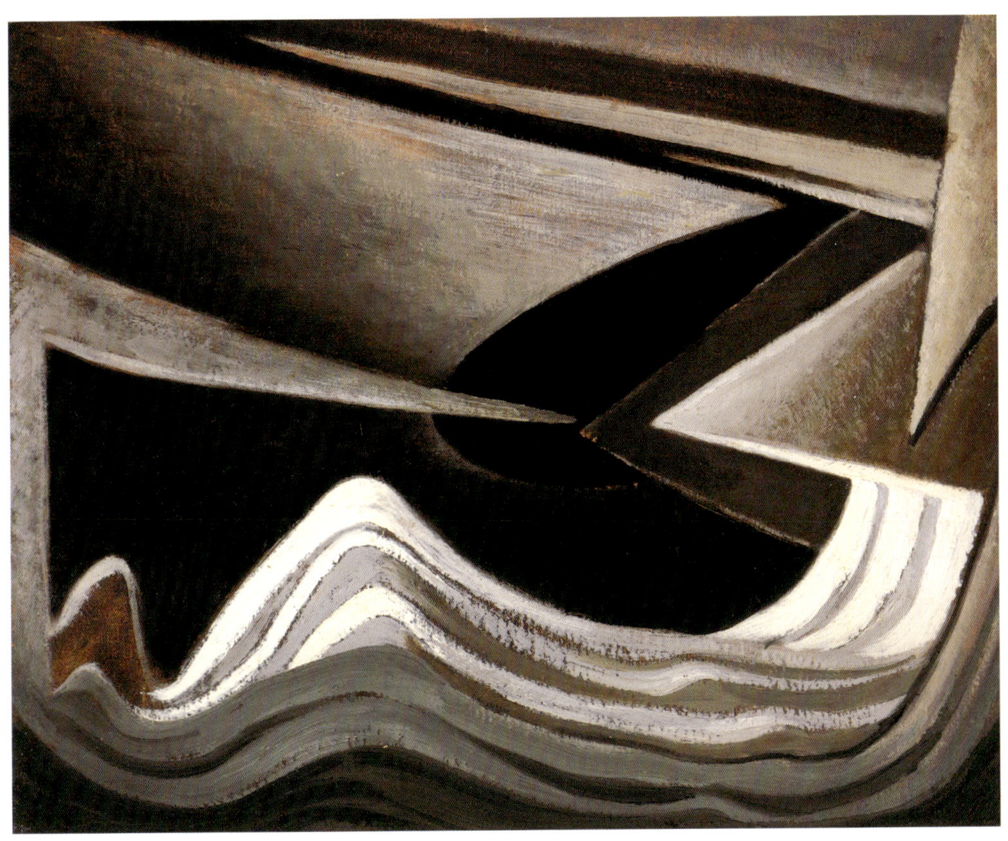

Edwin Holgate, 1892–1977

Baie des Moutons, Looking Northward, c. 1930 (Northern Quebec)

Holgate has trained his sights on the river in the early morning, surveying the scene as though from a nearby hill. The results, offered in a modernist format, are intriguing, from the light in the sky underneath the bank of cloud to the shining river and the outcropping of red rock.

Edwin Holgate
Oil on canvas, 63.3 x 76.1 cm
McMichael Canadian Art Collection, Kleinburg (1986.34)
Purchase, 1986

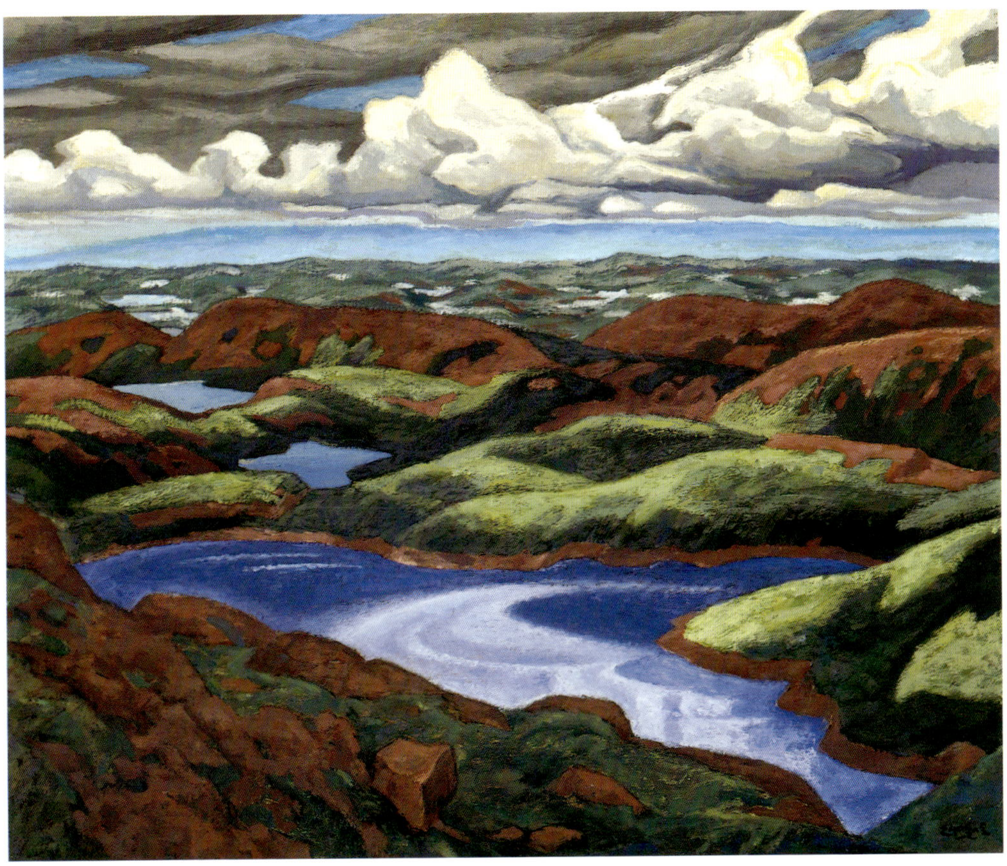

A.Y. Jackson, 1882–1974

The Red Maple, November 1914

This landscape is based on a sketch painted in the out-of-doors along the Oxtongue River that is in the McMichael Canadian Art Collection (1968.8.18). The river runs through the southwestern corner of Algonquin Park. In the foreground is a screen of red-leaved branches through which the viewer sees fast-flowing water turning into eddying rapids where the river narrows.

A.Y. Jackson
Oil on canvas, 82.0 x 99.5 cm
National Gallery of Canada, Ottawa (1038)
Purchase, 1914

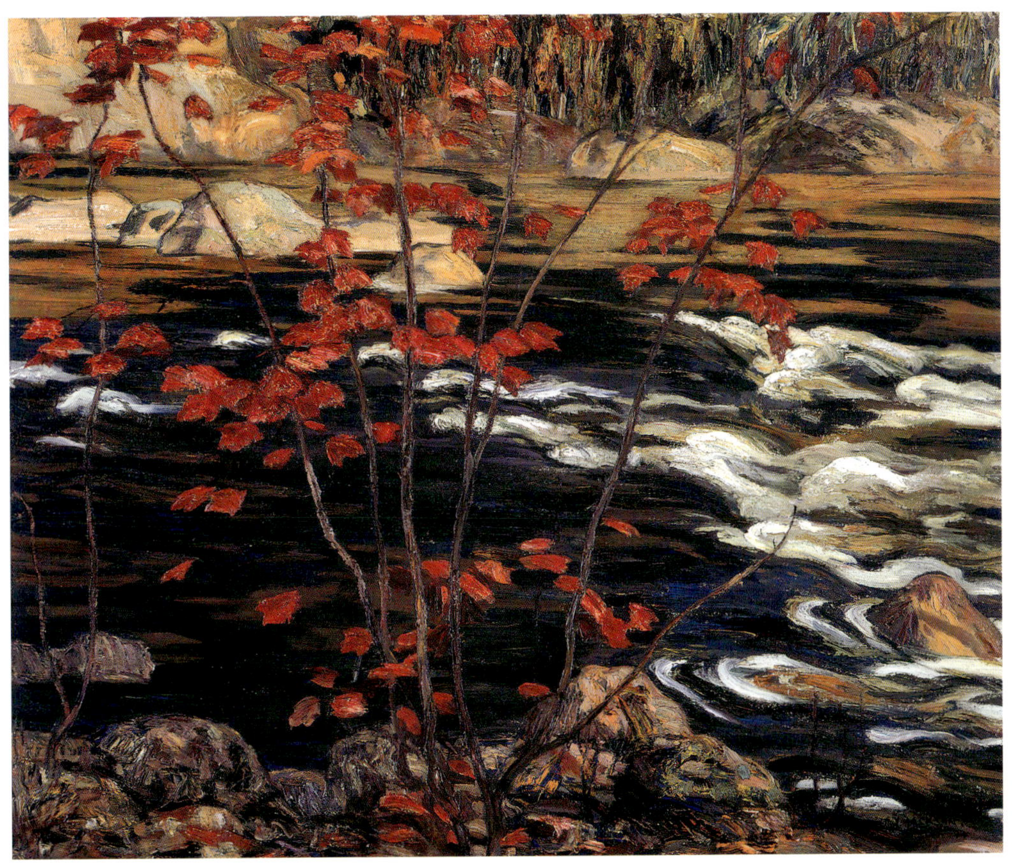

Autumn, Algoma, 1919

Jackson was interested in the rapidly flowing waters of Algoma. Note the contrast of the blues of the waters with the orange-reds of the autumn trees.

A.Y. Jackson

Oil on panel, 21.3 x 27.0 cm

McMichael Canadian Art Collection, Kleinburg (1968.8.13)

Gift of S. Walter Stewart

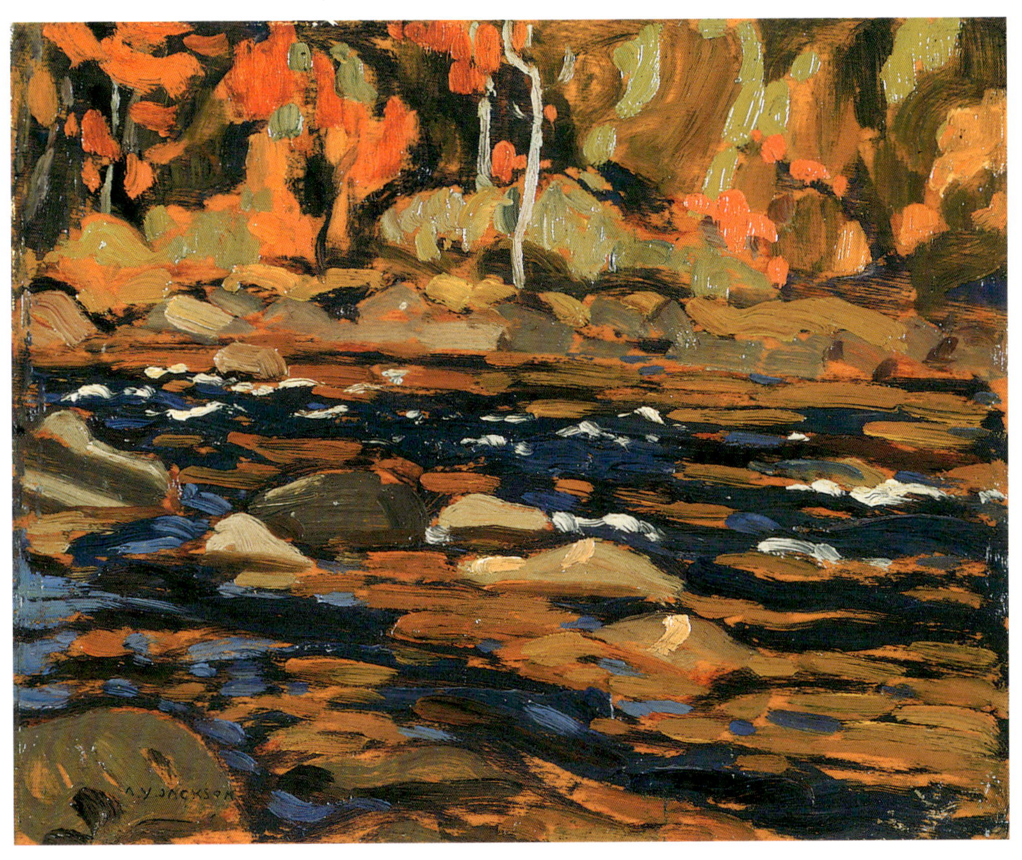
A.Y. JACKSON

October Morning, Algoma, 1920

Jackson wrote in his autobiography that it was in Algoma that he got the sketch for this canvas. He titled the oil sketch for the painting *Wartz Lake* (Vancouver Art Gallery Collection).

A.Y. Jackson

Oil on canvas, 126.3 x 151.7 cm

Hart House Permanent Collection, University of Toronto

Purchase, 1932

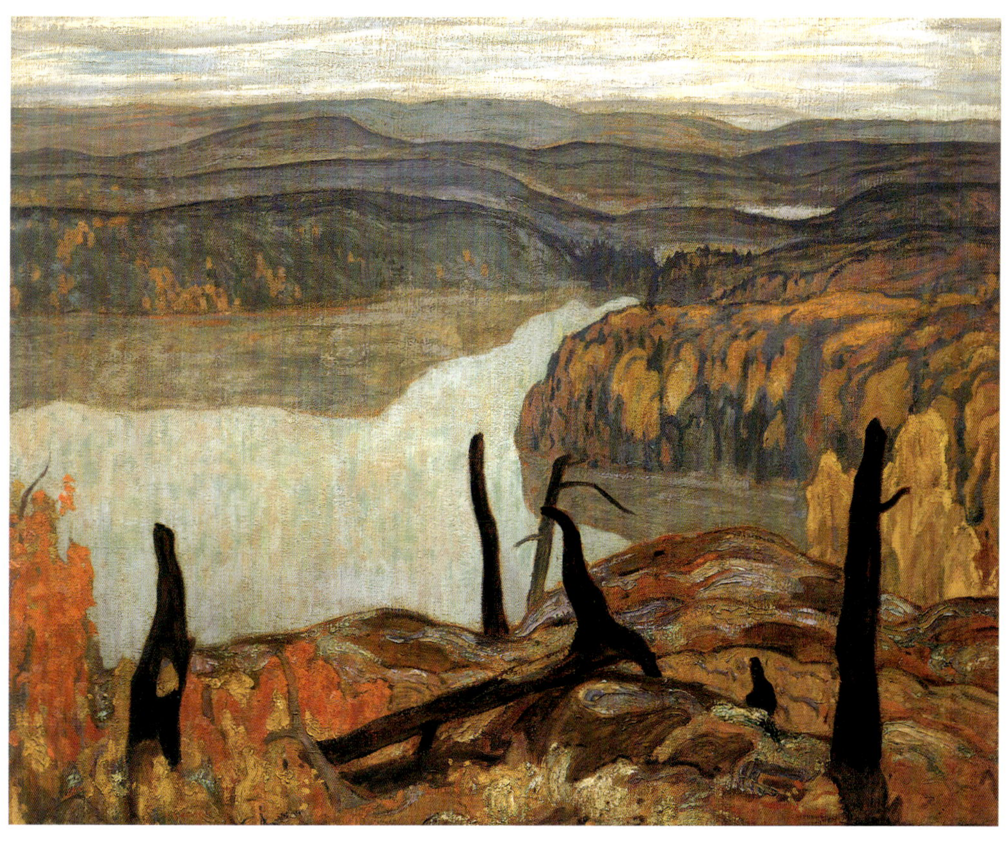

Waterfall, Algoma, 1921

Here Jackson has created an essay in structural form with rocks and waterfall boldly picked out.

A.Y. Jackson

Oil on panel, 21.7 x 26.8 cm

McMichael Canadian Art Collection, Kleinburg (1976.25.1)

Gift of the Founders, Robert and Signe McMichael

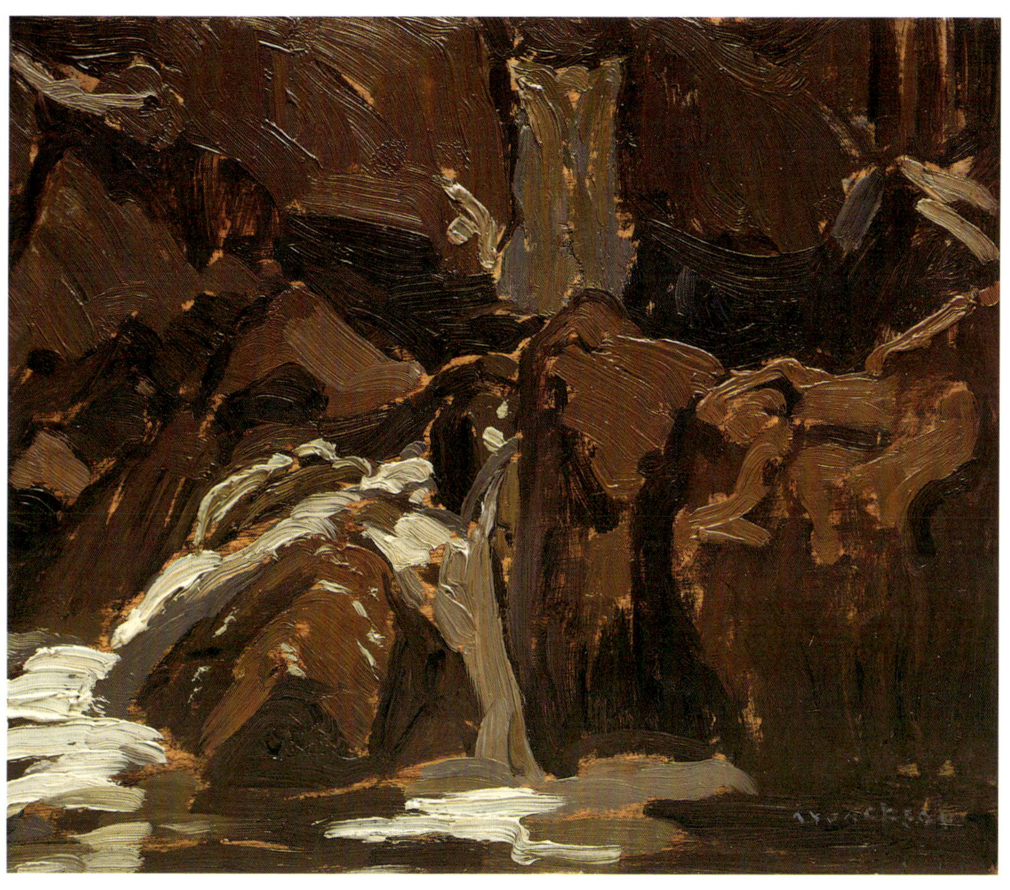

FRANK (FRANZ) H. JOHNSTON, 1888–1949

CANYON, ALGOMA, C. 1918

Like Jackson in *Waterfall, Algoma* (see page 75), Johnston has created a melody in dark colours. For Johnston what mattered was the contrast in colour and shape of the ancient rocks and gently splashing water. The sketch delicately evokes evening light.

Frank (Franz) H. Johnston
Gouache on cardboard, 23.3 x 23.5 cm
Art Gallery of Ontario, Toronto (51/6)
Gift of F.H. Brigden, 1951

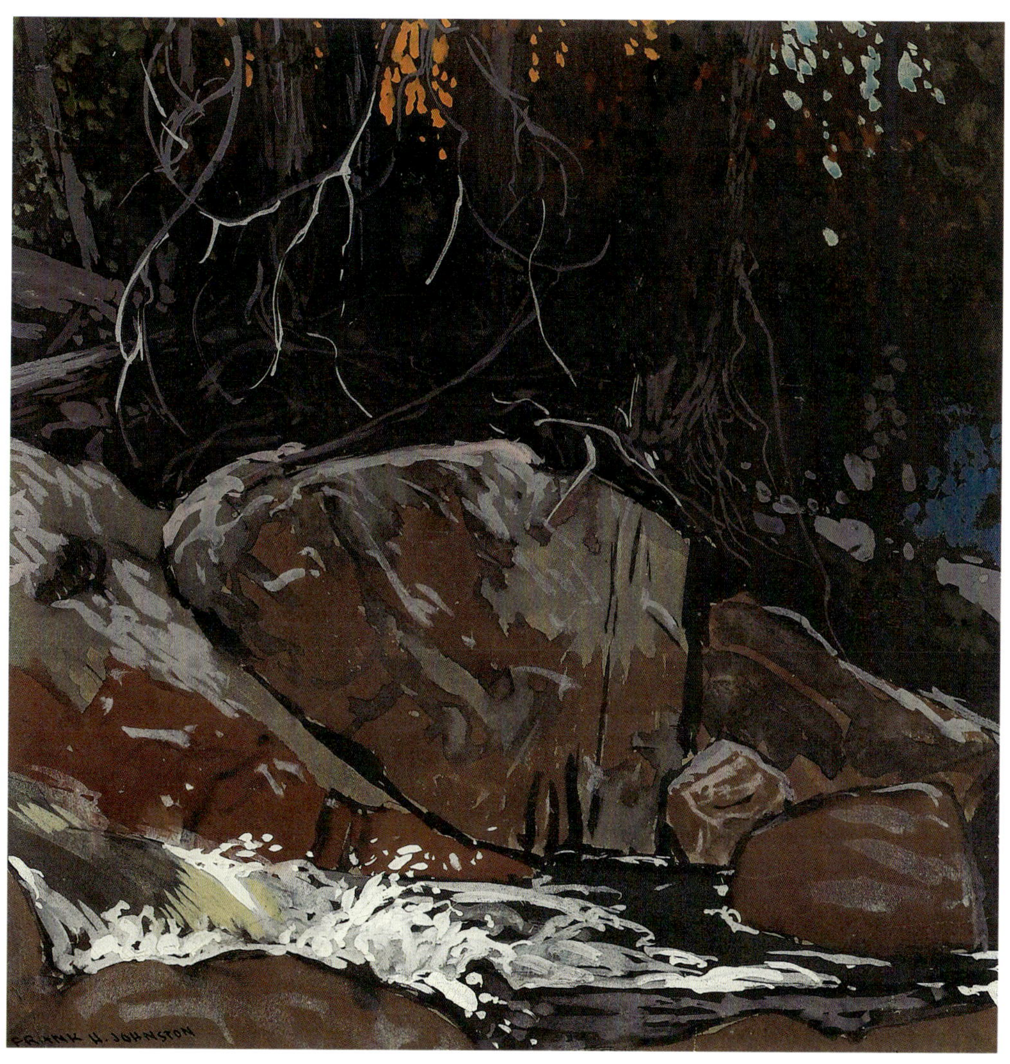
FRANK H. JOHNSTON

Montreal River, Algoma, 1919

This painting, possibly shown in the first "Group of Seven Exhibition of Paintings" in May 1920 as *Froth Pattern, Below Rapids*, conveys the excitement felt by Johnston on the boxcar trips. He seems to have been the only one of the group who recorded scenes of the 1919 trip using gouache, a medium often used by commercial artists and earlier by Tom Thomson. The technique allowed him to capture an effect of spontaneity, so that the viewer almost feels as though the waves of the Montreal River tumble immediately before him or her.

Frank (Franz) H. Johnston
Gouache on paper, 36.2 x 34.8 cm
Private Collection, Toronto

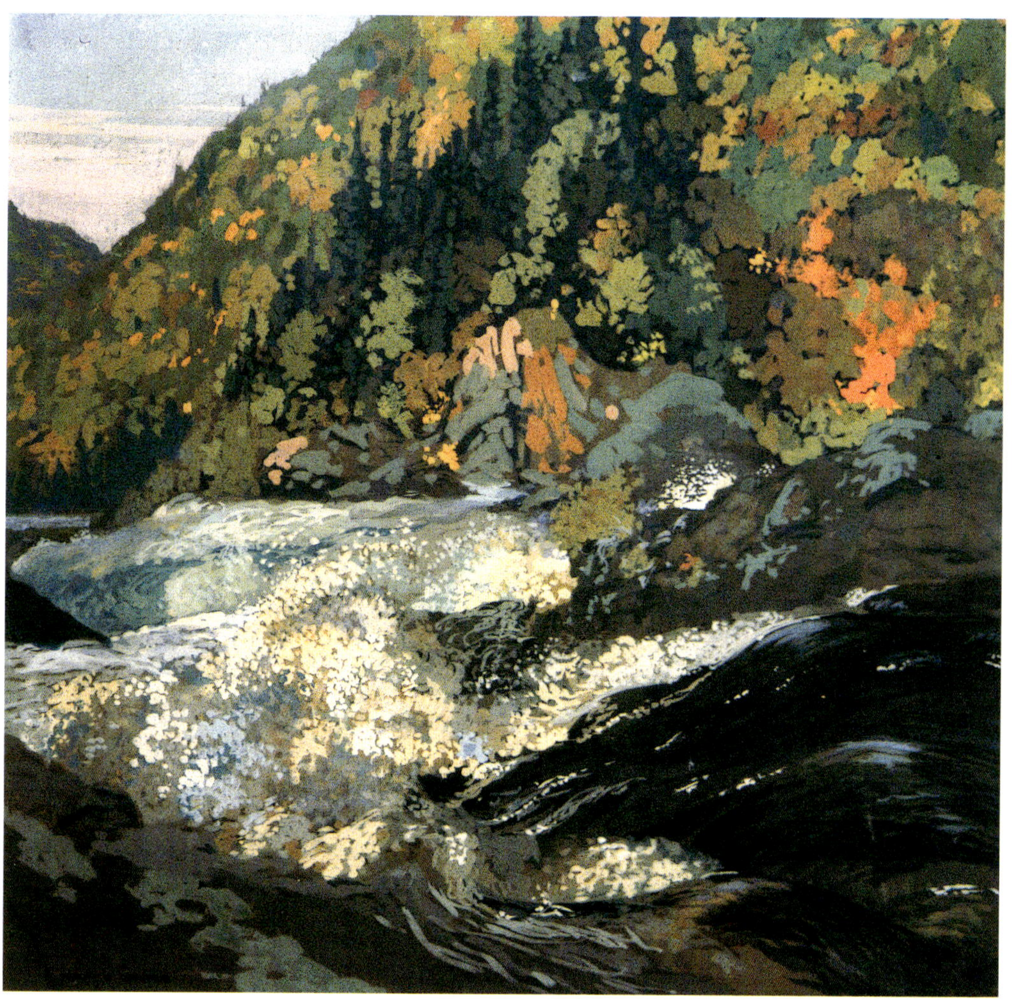

Little Falls, Algoma, c. 1919

In this lucidly designed sketch, probably painted in Algoma, Johnston shows the influence of MacDonald's bold handling.

Frank (Franz) H. Johnston
Oil on panel, 19.0 x 14.0 cm
Tom Thomson Memorial Art Gallery, Owen Sound (999.001.09)
Gift of the Estate of Jennings David Young, 1999

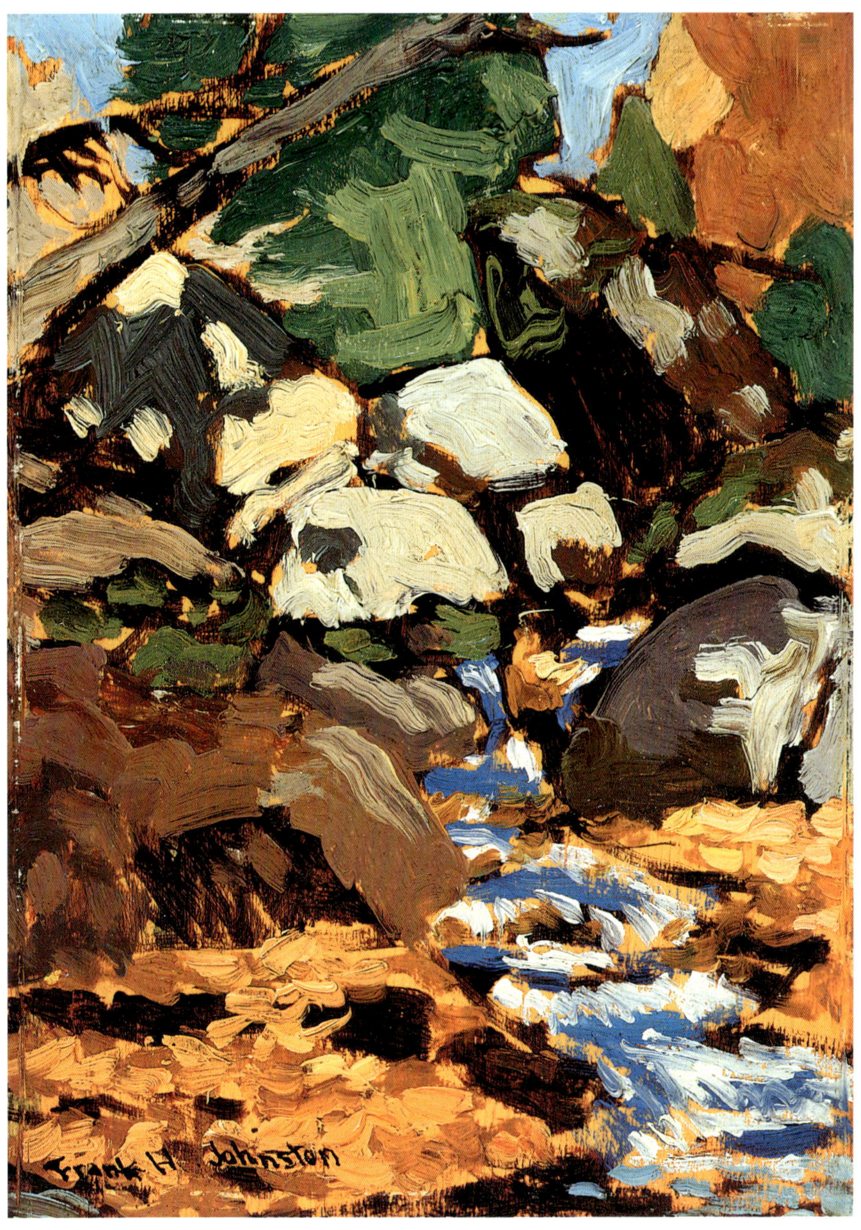
Frank H Johnston

The Awakening: Spring on the Nipigon River, c. 1926

One of Johnston's happiest themes was the spring waters, here painted in April, as the artist wrote in a note on the back. He also noted the exact location: about a mile from the town of Nipigon, Ontario, and about one hundred miles from Fort William. In other works, he titled the theme "Spring Rhapsody" and something of the season's evocative power appears in the lyrical colours of the water, which contrast gently with the snow that still remains on the riverbanks.

Frank (Franz) H. Johnston
Oil on board, 40.6 x 50.8 cm
Private Collection

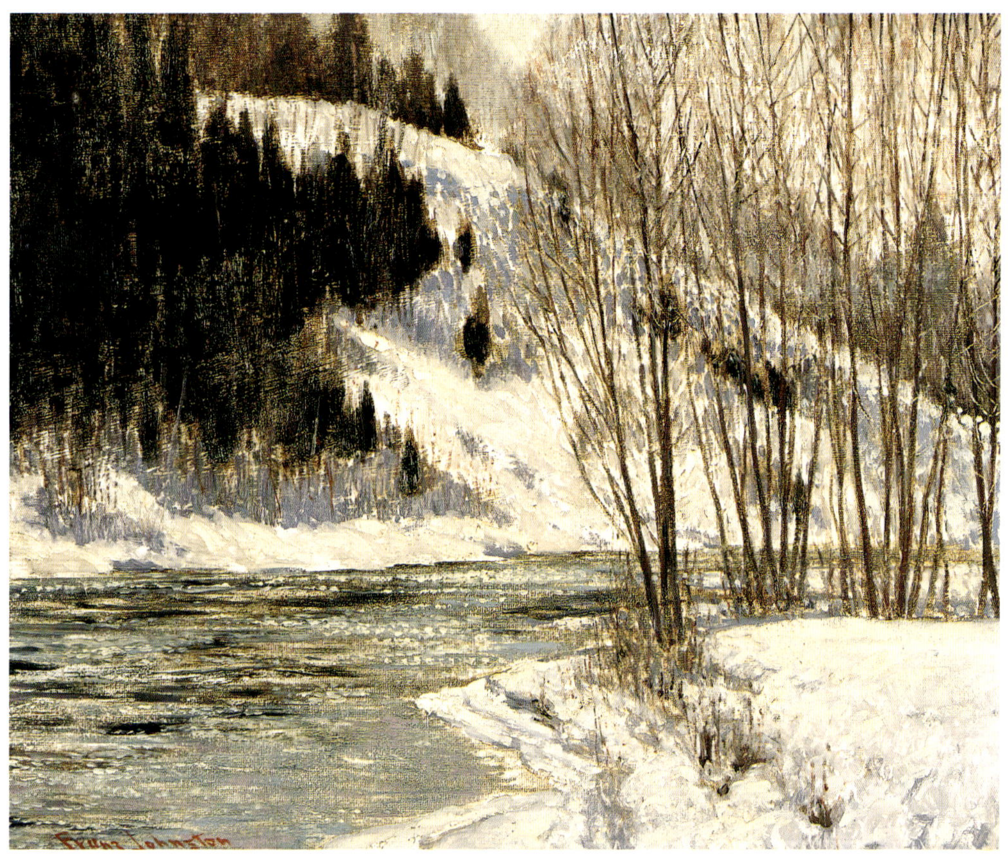

Arthur Lismer, 1885–1969

Georgian Bay, 1913

Lismer's vision of Georgian Bay provides a brisk, buoyant overview of the role of water and sky in the north. The day is overclouded, but the racing water gives the scene an irresistible gaiety.

Arthur Lismer
Oil on board, 22.9 x 30.3 cm
Private Collection, Winnipeg

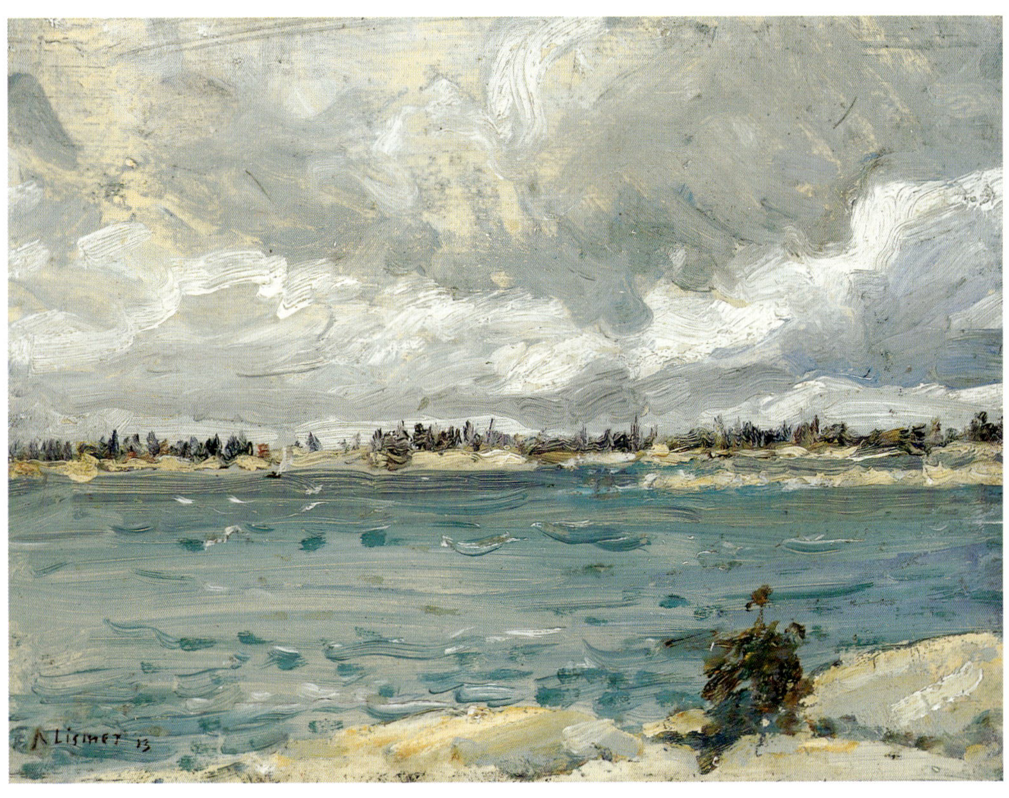
A Lismer '13

Sackville River, 1917

Water was a subject with a powerful hold on the imagination, as Lismer demonstrates in this lively painting, likely influenced by his knowledge of works by Thomson and MacDonald. As though to underscore this influence, Lismer even introduces a Thomson-like tree in the foreground. Unlike the painter Carmichael, however, who painted as though he stood in midstream, Lismer painted from a particular vantage point on a rocky hillside. The water in this work is the story: splashy, and full of excitement and colour.

The Sackville River is located in Nova Scotia near Halifax, where Lismer worked as principal of the Victoria School of Art and Design from 1916 to 1919.

Arthur Lismer
Oil on canvas, 77.2 x 92.4 cm
Art Gallery of Nova Scotia, Halifax (1925.2)
Purchased, 1919

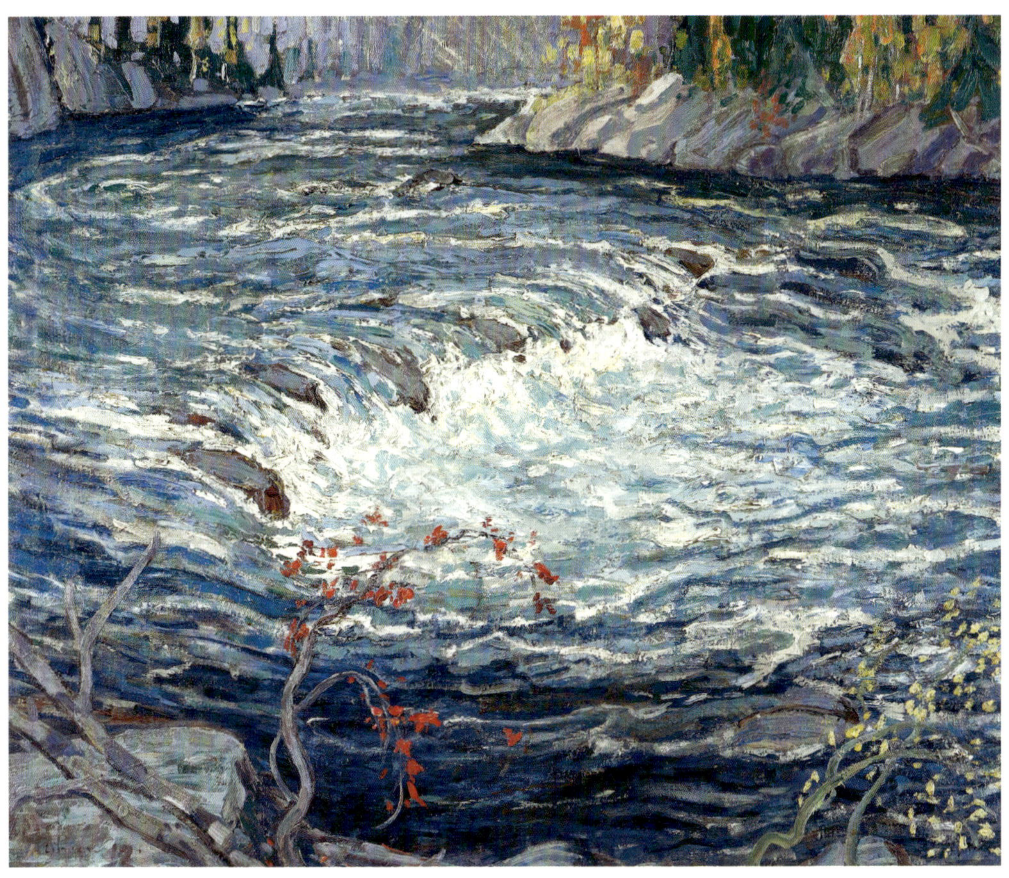

J.E.H. MacDonald, 1873–1932

Spring Rapids, 1912 (Magnetawan River near Burk's Falls)

The waters of blue, grey, and pink fall in swirling rapids of yellow, white, and blue, which seem to flow towards the viewer.

J.E.H. MacDonald
Oil on cardboard, 17.7 x 22.8 cm
National Gallery of Canada, Ottawa (4740)
Bequest of Dr. J.M. MacCallum, Toronto, 1944

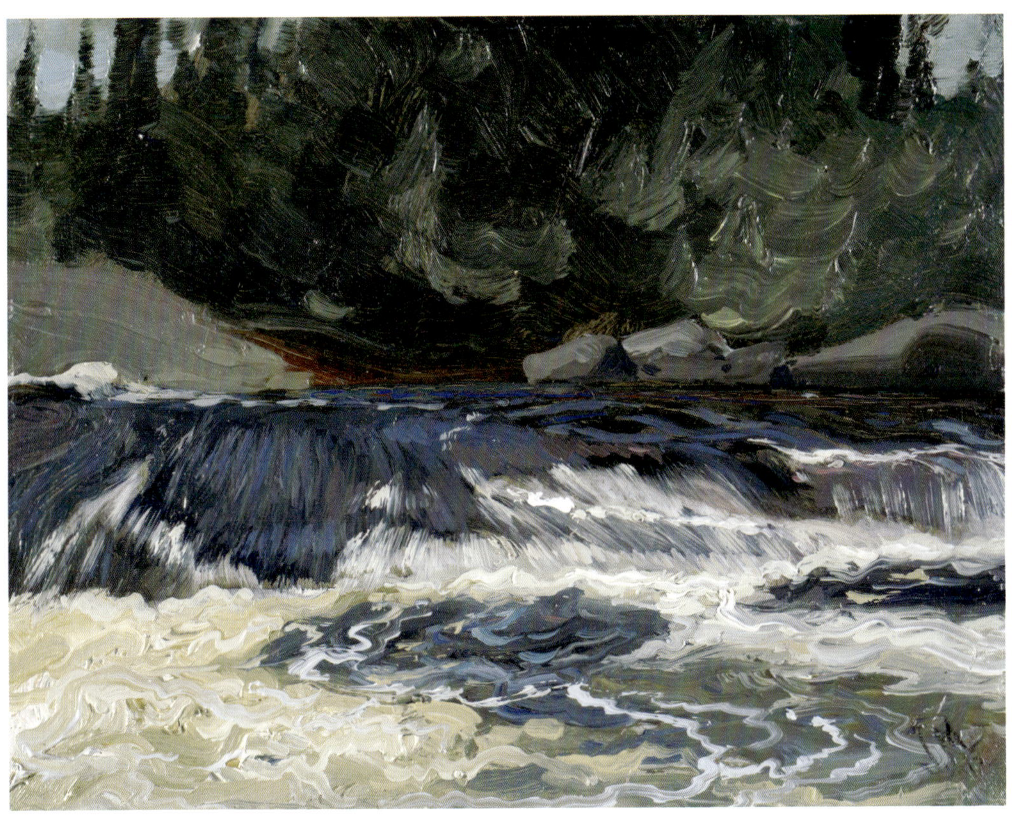

A Rapid in the North, 1913

Here the briskly flowing waters have different depths, from deep black interlaced with blue to shallow near the rock and golden in the sunlight. In the background, the rich colouring to the leaves (browns, reds, oranges, greens), thickly laid down in impastoed strokes, suggests that the season is autumn.

J.E.H. MacDonald
Oil on canvas, 51.4 x 72.1 cm
Art Gallery of Hamilton

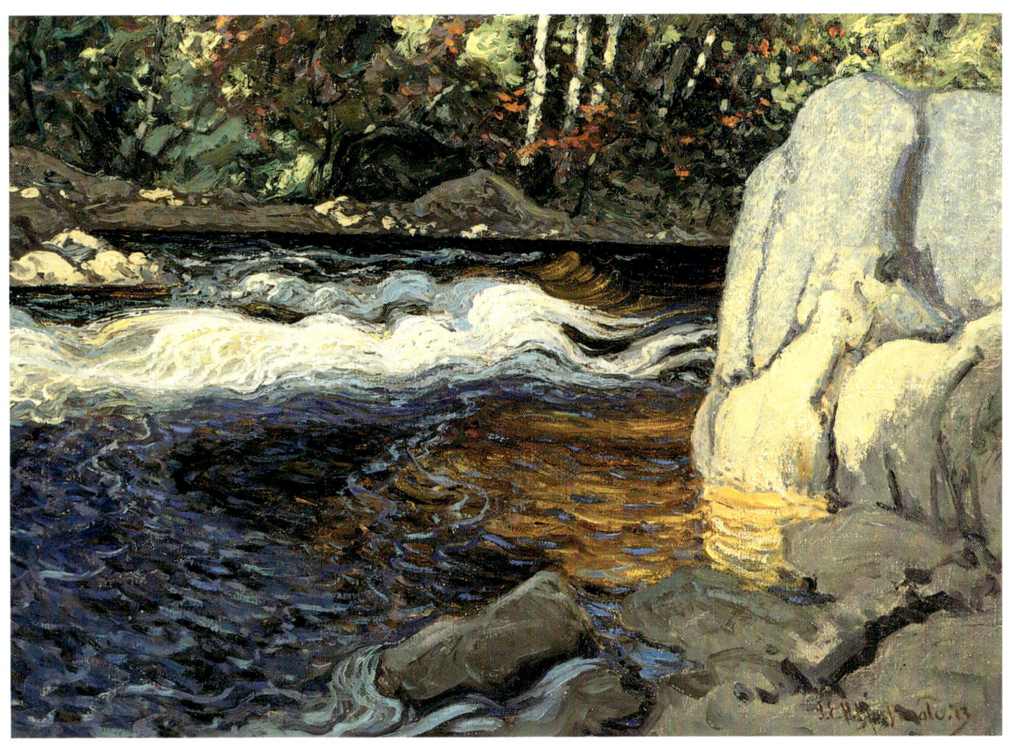

Leaves in the Brook, 1919

Clearly, MacDonald was fascinated with the way the water flows peacefully, creating a complex, interlacing pattern with many deep central pools.

J.E.H. MacDonald
Oil on canvas, 52.7 x 65.0 cm
McMichael Canadian Art Collection, Kleinburg (1966.16.35)
Gift of the Founders, Robert and Signe McMichael

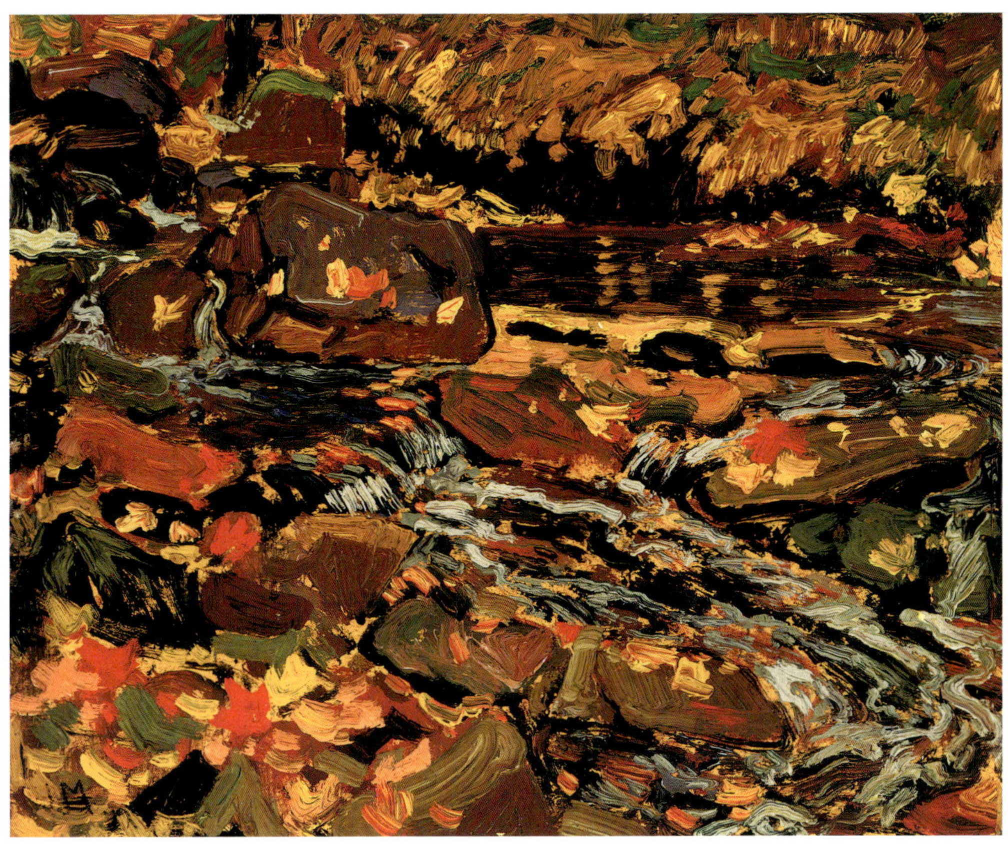

Falls, Montreal River, 1920

The year 1917 was a shattering time for MacDonald; he had what seems to have been a stroke that year. But by 1920, he was painting this smouldering image of the Canadian North, with its brilliant autumn colours and tumbling waters. The painting rephrased and amplified his *The Wild River* of 1919, which had challenged critics; but now the viewer's eye is drawn in a diagonal along the path of the waters into the distance and towards an open patch of sky. The colours in this painting offer dazzling contrasts (note the lime and pink of the rocks in the foreground), and the brushwork is dashingly handled. MacDonald positioned himself on a promontory in the foreground to paint the sketch – water seems to bounce beyond the artist (and the viewer) at left to disappear in the picture in a spiralling middle section of the canvas. MacDonald must have drawn energy from nature. Characteristically, in his landscape the placement of the horizon near the top of the canvas induces the viewer's eye to rest upon the centre of the composition in the midst of vigorous waters. These tumultuous spaces help to emotionally and physically renew the viewer, liberating the spirit. Likely, MacDonald's readings in Eastern philosophy had reaffirmed the idea of a spiritual energy immanent in nature; he would have had awareness of this from his Presbyterian upbringing and his interest in Christian Science. He would have known, for instance, of Mary Baker Eddy, the founder of Christian Science (she was one of the people Jackson remembered discussing in the boxcar), who regarded "Wilderness" as an entryway to the unfolding of the great facts of existence.

J.E.H. MacDonald
Oil on canvas, 121.9 x 153.0 cm
Art Gallery of Ontario, Toronto (2109)
Purchased, 1933

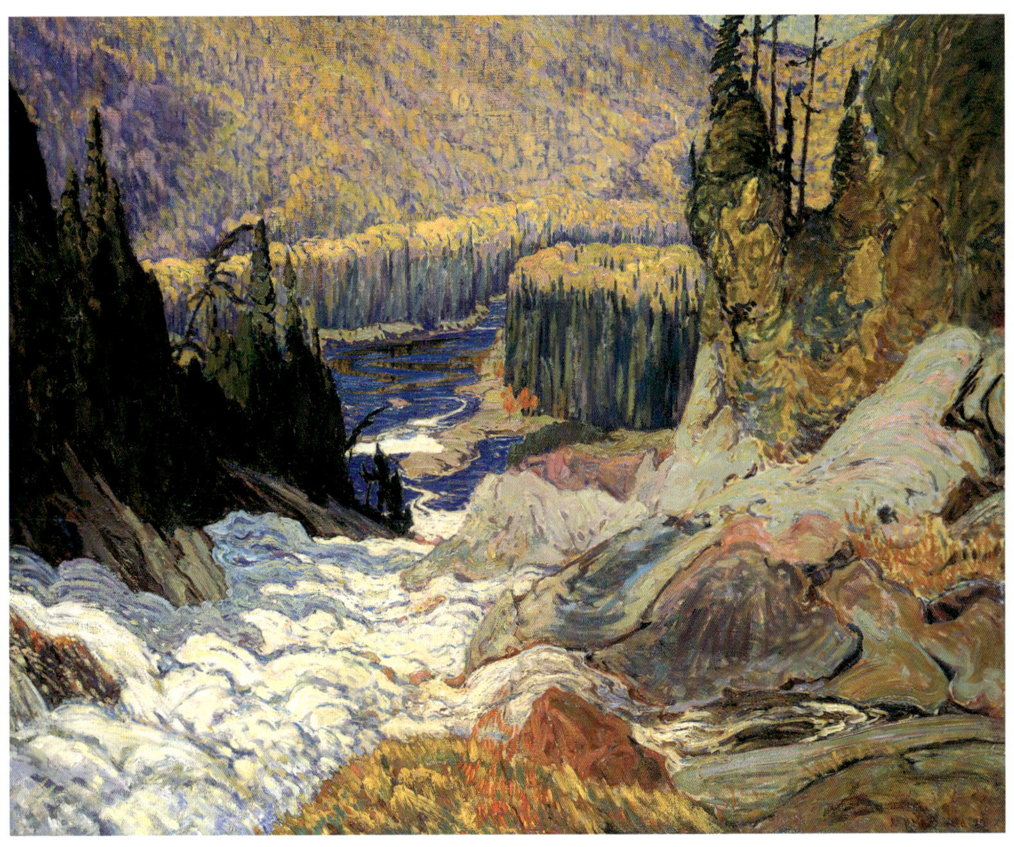

Algoma Waterfall, 1920

To this painting, one of his spirited essays on the subject of waterfalls in Algoma, MacDonald brought an undiminished vigour and a willingness to experiment. Here the viewer stands in the woods at the bottom of several sets of waterfalls, looking at them through autumn foliage. It is dusk, as we can see from the darkening sky. MacDonald owned a photograph of the scene (see page 5).

J.E.H. MacDonald

Oil on canvas, 76.3 x 88.5 cm

McMichael Canadian Art Collection, Kleinburg (1968.7.2)

Gift of Col. R.S. McLaughlin, 1968

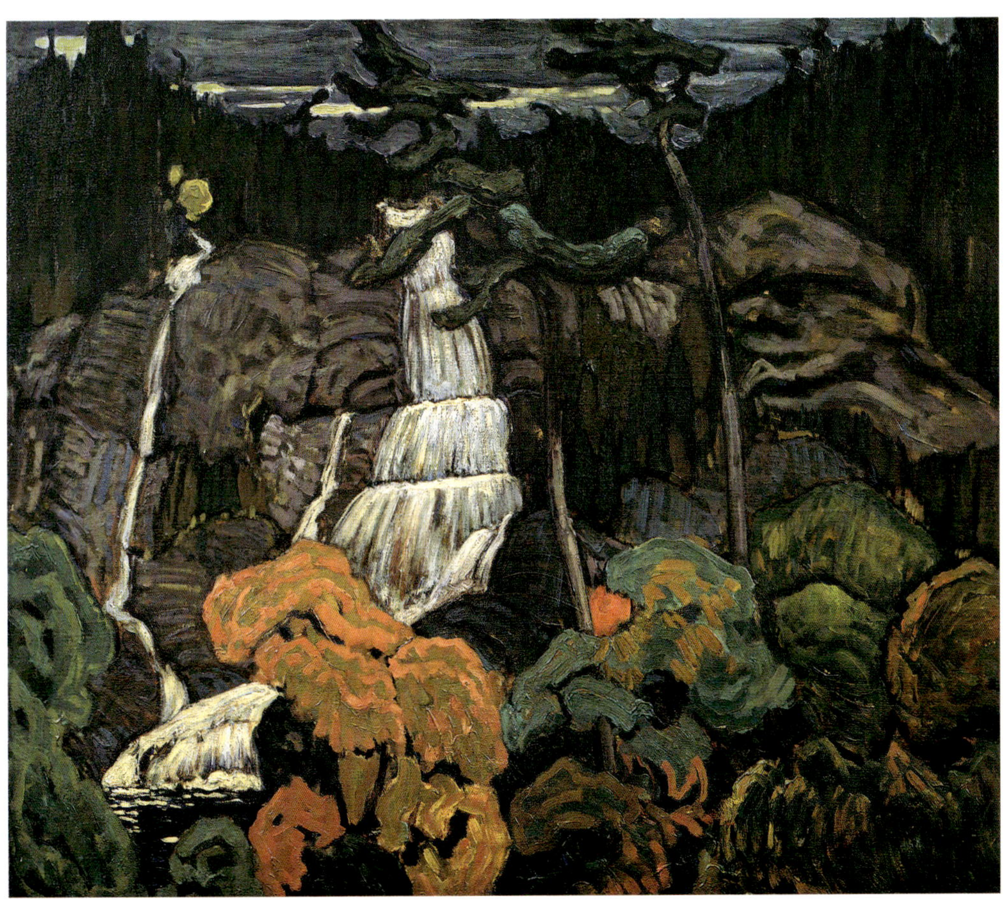

Batchawana Rapid, 1920

The painting has bold brushwork and brilliantly handled colour, particularly in the pink and green sunlit rocks and the tumbling, shadowy water. Note the way MacDonald suggested contrasts: to the right of the surging water is a still pool.

J.E.H. MacDonald
Oil on canvas, 71.9 x 91.9 cm
National Gallery of Canada, Ottawa (3538)
Purchased, 1928

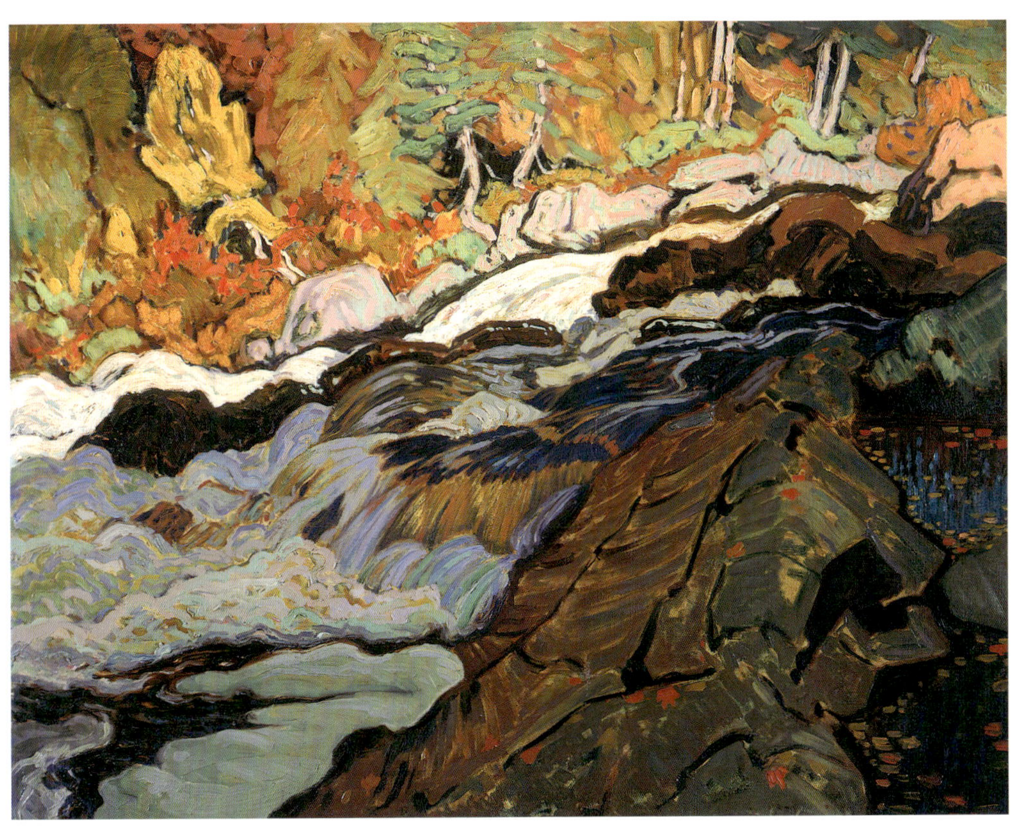

The Solemn Land, 1921 (Montreal River)

The weather was sometimes overcast when MacDonald painted Algoma's Montreal River, but he still managed to capture the momentary effect of a gleam of light on the hills. The colour brought out by the light strikes a bold note in an otherwise sombre scene.

J.E.H. MacDonald
Oil on canvas, 122.5 x 153.5 cm
National Gallery of Canada, Ottawa (1785)
Purchased, 1921

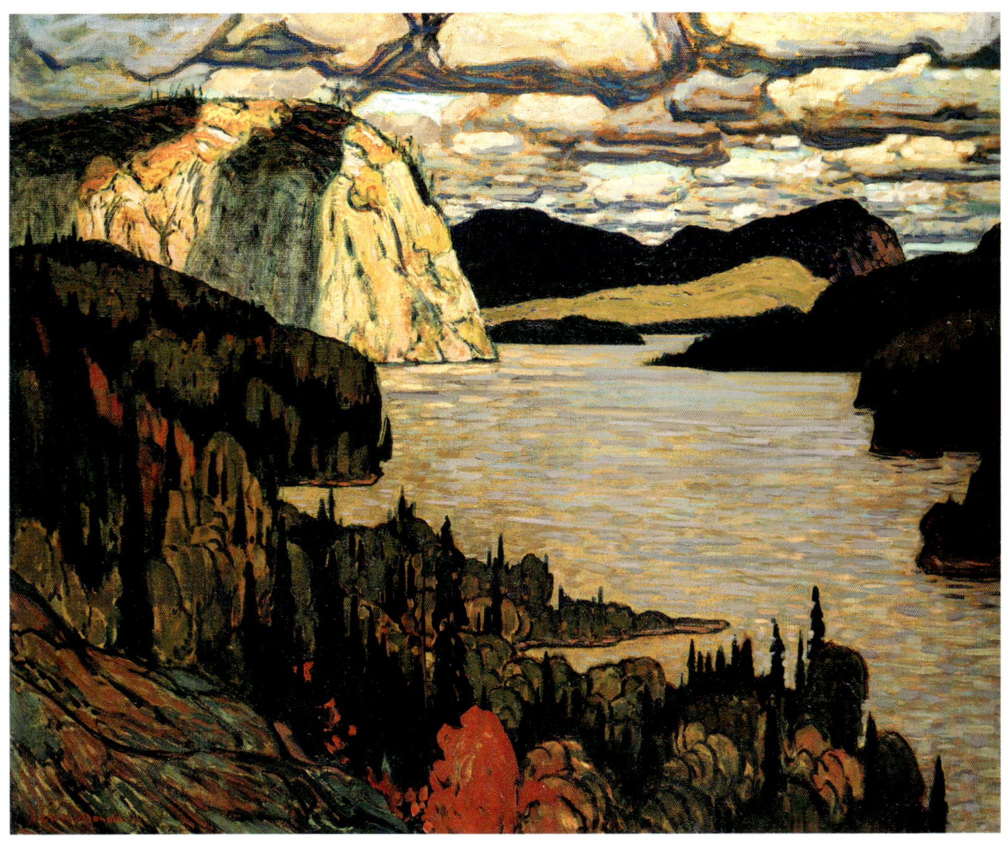

Mist Fantasy, Sand River, Algoma, 1920

MacDonald approached abstraction in his summary handling in this beautiful sketch.

J.E.H. MacDonald
Oil on cardboard, 21.4 x 26.6 cm
National Gallery of Canada, Ottawa (4858)
Purchased, 1947

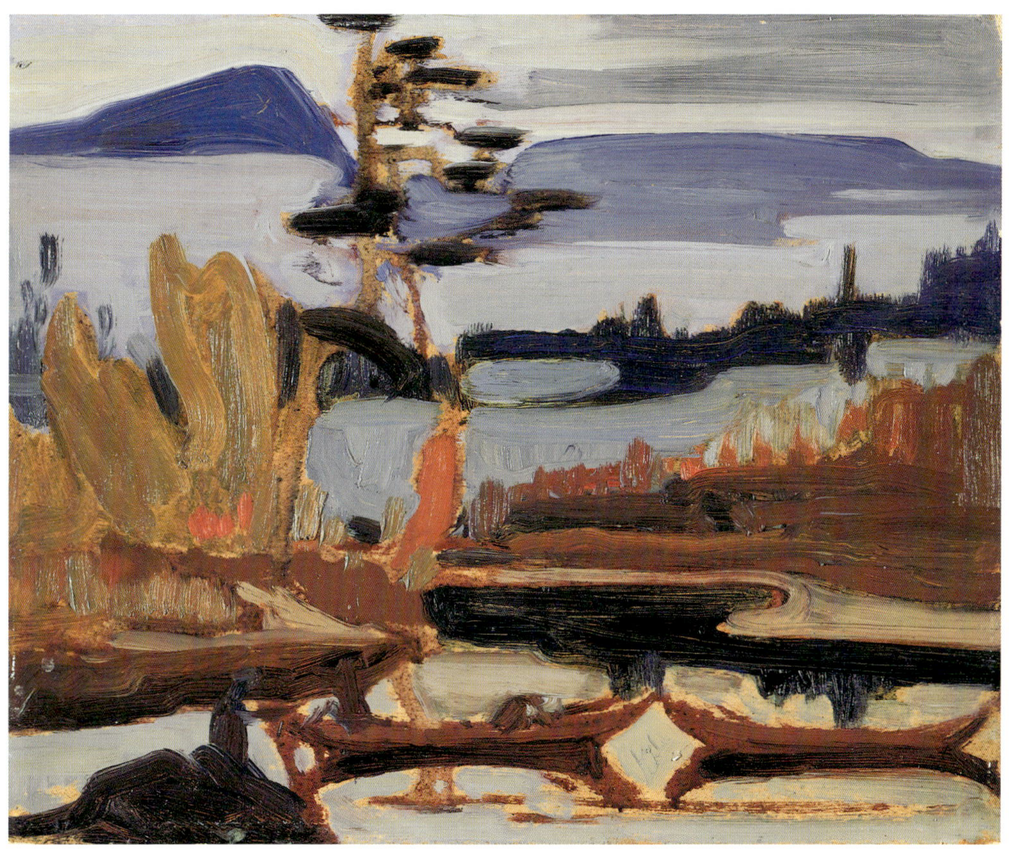

Mist Fantasy, Northland, 1922

MacDonald's last trip to Algoma was in 1920, but he continued to draw upon his experiences after that; paintings such as this one condense and express his delight in the scenery he loved. Note the many changes from the sketch (see page 103). All MacDonald's work is marked by formal inventiveness (note the way the mist appears under and amongst the blue hills) and highly expressive qualities. Here he has painted a work that hovers on the metaphorical to become a symbol of the Canadian North.

J.E.H. MacDonald

Oil on canvas, 53.7 x 66.7 cm

Art Gallery of Ontario, Toronto (899)

Gift of Mrs. S.J. Williams, Toronto, in memory of F. Elinor Williams, 1927

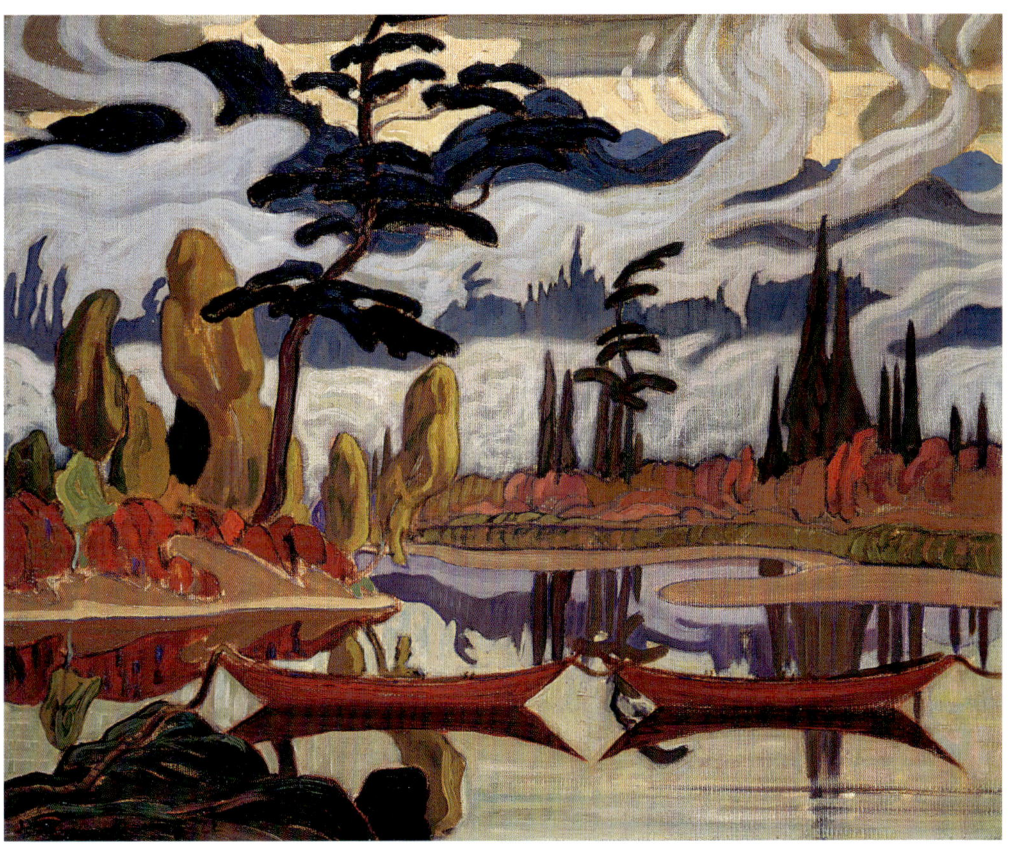

October Shower Gleam, 1922

When MacDonald first showed the painting, he titled it *October Shower Gleam*, *Telegram Lake* after the conservative newspaper in Toronto, the *Telegram*, that had criticized the Group.

J.E.H. MacDonald
Oil on canvas, 105.4 x 120.7 cm
Hart House Permanent Collection, University of Toronto
Purchase with income from the Harold and Murray Wrong Memorial Fund, 1933

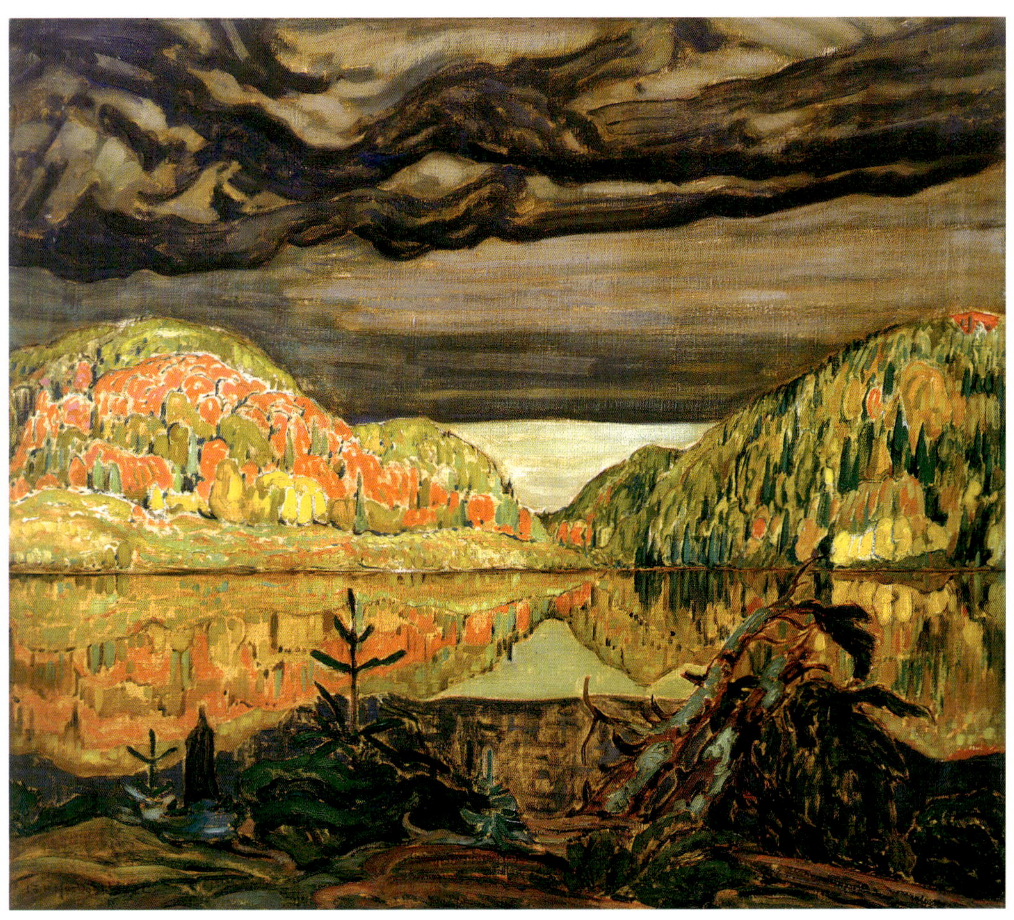

Tom Thomson, 1877–1917

Spring, French River, 1 June 1914

On the back of the sketch, someone, probably Dr. J.M. MacCallum, Thomson's patron and friend, wrote in ink, "Spring – French River – Tom Thomson/June 1/1914." MacCallum would have known the date so exactly because he and Thomson camped at French River on the way to MacCallum's cottage on Georgian Bay. MacCallum recorded this in his "Notes on Tom Thomson," around 2 May 1941 (Dr. James M. MacCallum Papers, Library and Archives, National Gallery of Canada, Ottawa). The sketch has a delicate coloration, ranging from browns to purple.

Tom Thomson
Oil on plywood, 21.6 x 26.9 cm
National Gallery of Canada, Ottawa (4657)
Bequest of Dr. J.M. MacCallum, Toronto, 1944

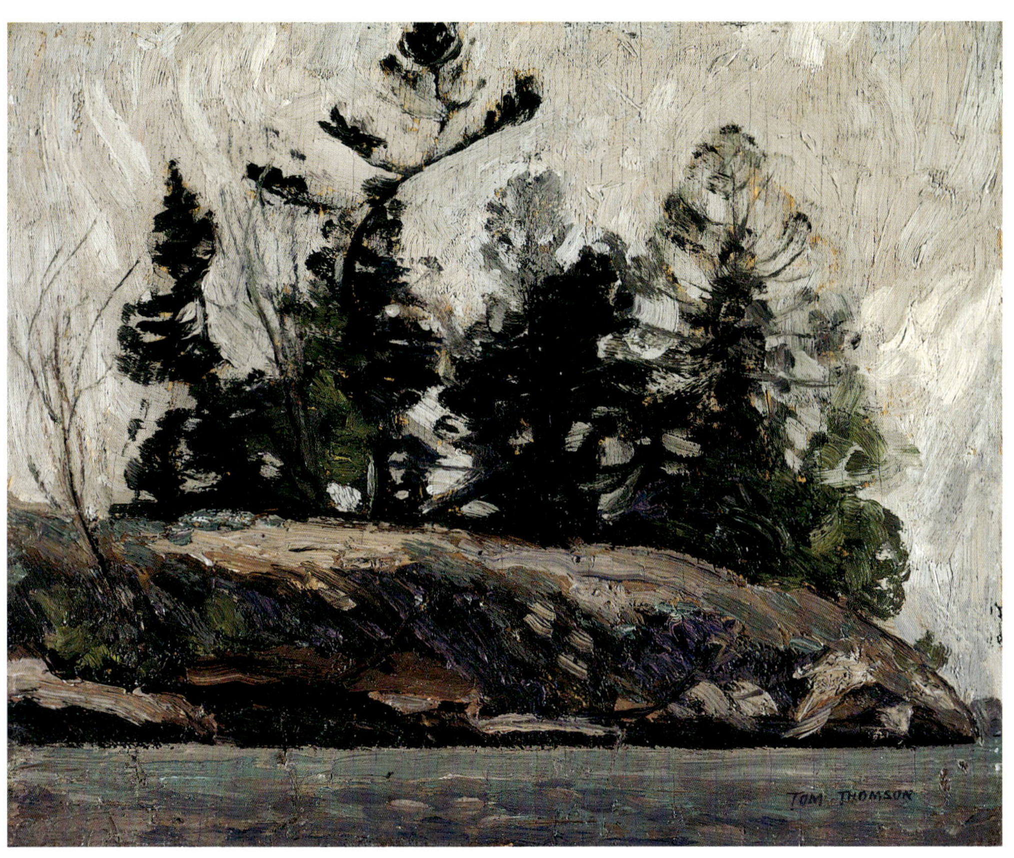
TOM THOMSON

NORTHERN RIVER, WINTER 1914–1915

The dominant colour of the painting is black. Thomson called the painting his "swamp picture" in a letter to Dr. MacCallum on 22 April 1915 (Dr. James M. MacCallum Papers, Library and Archives, National Gallery of Canada, Ottawa).

Tom Thomson

Oil on canvas, 115.1 x 102.0 cm

National Gallery of Canada, Ottawa (1055)

Purchased from the artist through the Ontario Society of Artists, 1915

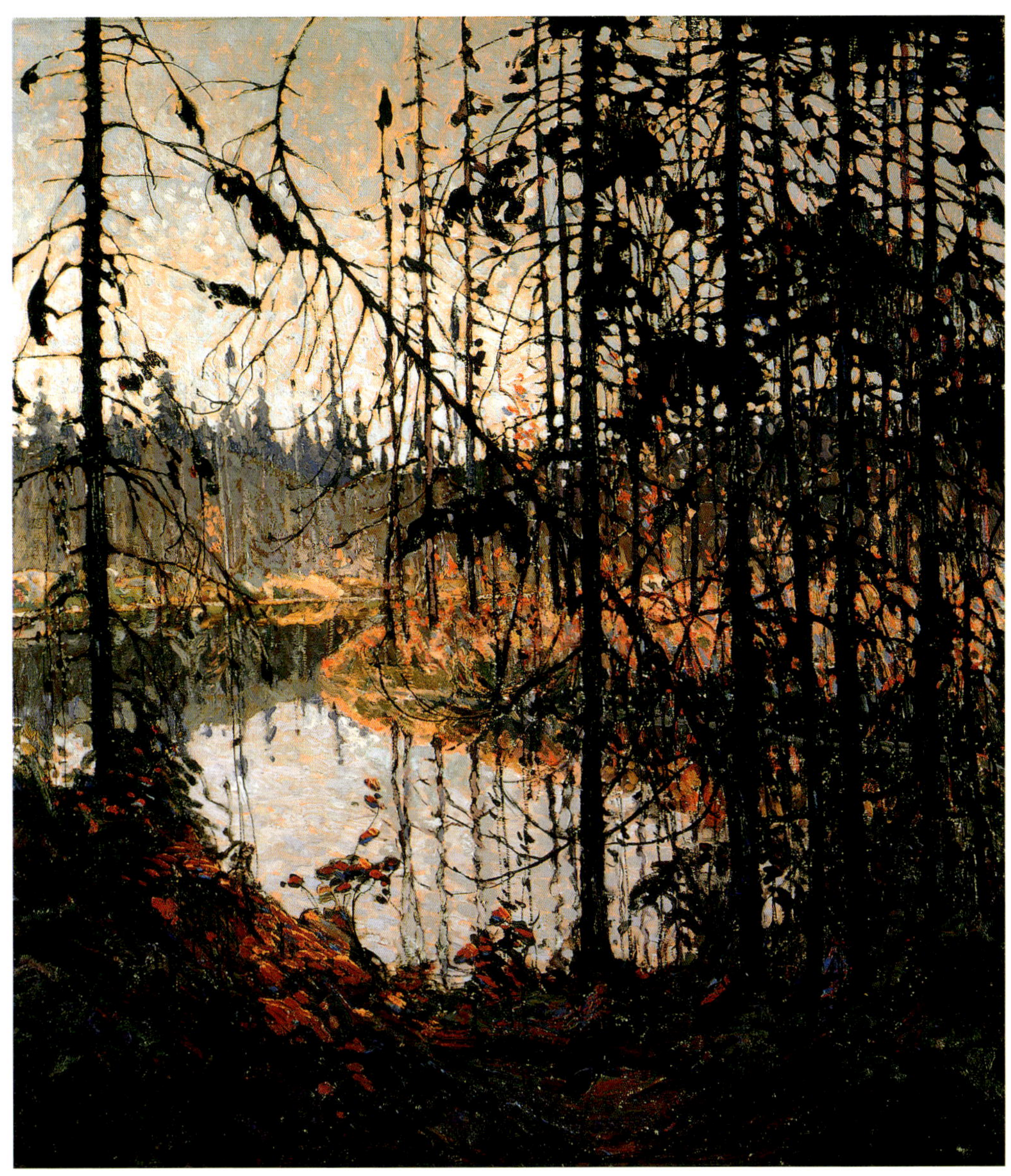

River, March–April 1915

In the spring of 1915, Thomson painted many sketches that showed the "opening of the waters," one of which was this sketch and one of which he worked up into his famous painting *Spring Ice* (National Gallery of Canada, Ottawa). Since there is still ice on the lake in this sketch, it was probably painted earlier in the year than the sketch for *Spring Ice*. Thomson wrote Dr. MacCallum in his letter of April 22 that the ice was still on the lakes but was getting rotten. This sketch could have been painted close to that date. In the sky, Thomson used turquoise, yellow, and lavender to indicate the close of the day.

Tom Thomson

Oil on wood, 21.2 x 26.5 cm

National Gallery of Canada, Ottawa (1538)

Purchase, 1918

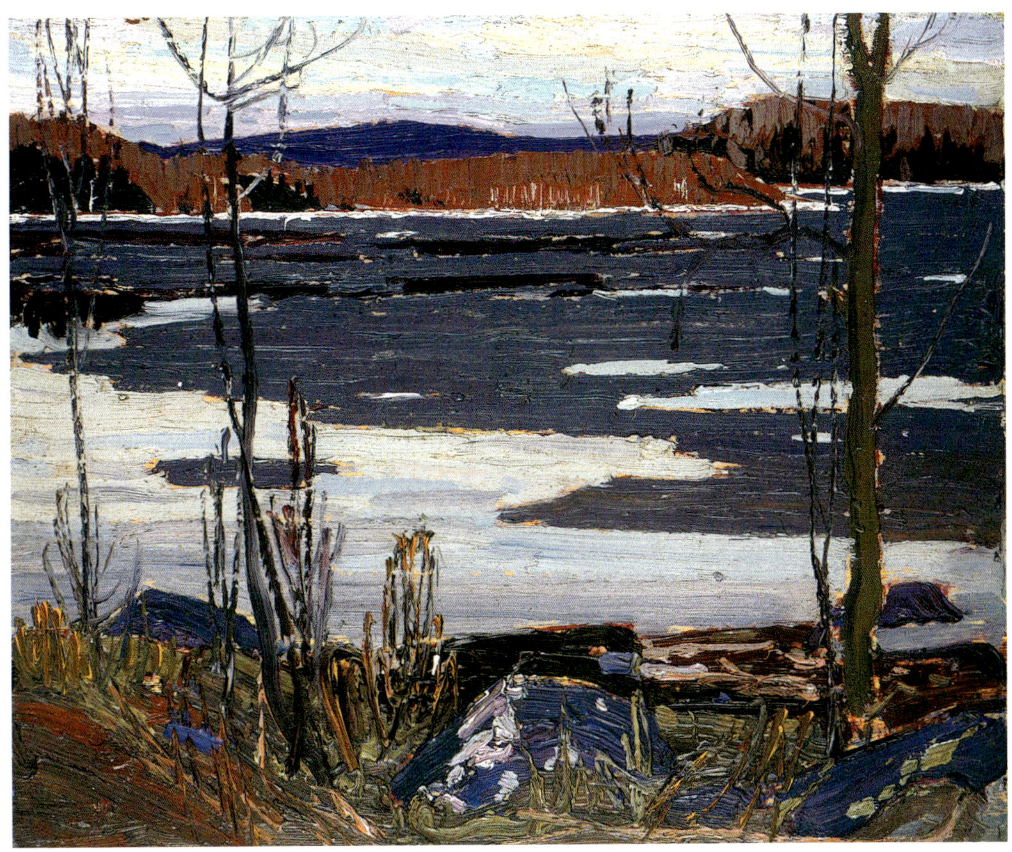

Spring Foliage on the Muskoka River, Spring 1916

On the back of this sketch, MacCallum wrote "a very good example of success [sureness?] of brush stroke." Thomson here focused on a small section of the river, framing the view of the splashing water with sage green foliage and crisply painted dark rocks.

Tom Thomson

Oil on wood, 21.5 x 26.7 cm

McMichael Canadian Art Collection, Kleinburg (1970.1.3)

Purchased with funds donated by R.A. Laidlaw, Toronto, 1969

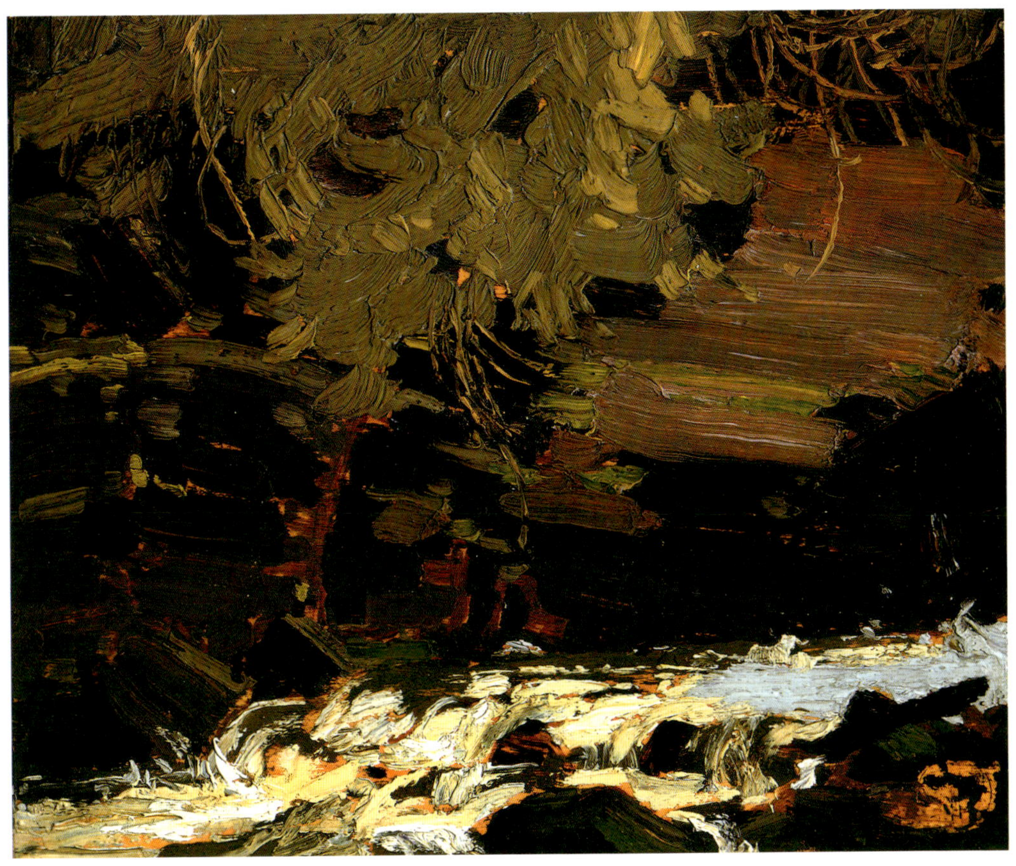

F.H. Varley, 1881–1969

Ottawa River, c. 1943

Varley has introduced a transcendental feeling into the theme of rivers with this painting: the island seems to float in the midst of the waters, while on the shore an artist records the scene. Curator Christopher Varley has suggested that Varley's love of J.M. Turner (1775–1851), the most successful of the English painters of his day, was evident in the painting. Turner was an artist from whom Varley borrowed motifs quite consciously during the last thirty years of his life, but always adding his own point of view.

F.H. Varley
Oil on canvas, 55.88 x 71.12 cm
Private Collection, Vancouver

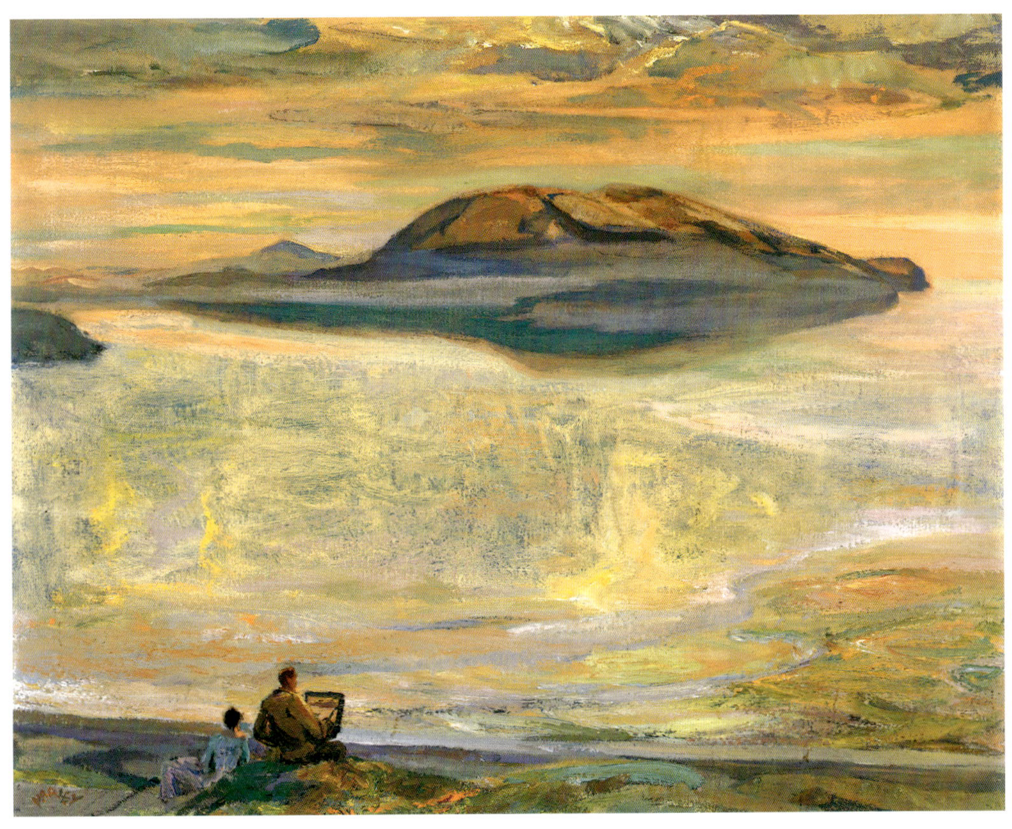

Appendix

The first three excerpts are taken from letters written by Lawren Harris to J.E.H. MacDonald, and they discuss the organization of the boxcar trip. They are included courtesy of the National Archives of Canada, Ottawa, the J.E.H. MacDonald Papers, MG30 (D111).

✧✧✧

Undated (August 1918?)
"Woodend"
R.R.1, Allandale, Ont.

Dear Jim,
...The trip – overnight on C.P.R. to the Soo. Next day at the Soo we enter a caboose which will be our home while in the North. Said caboose is hitched onto some train or other hauled to a siding in the Agawa Canyon 120 miles north of the Soo and left there for two or three days while we proceed to get a strangle hold on the surroundings. From mile 120 we are picked up by a down-going train and left on another siding for a few days and again picked up and left on still another siding and so on until we land in the Soo with a mass of sketches and C.P.R. ourselves home again...

✧✧✧

Sept. (1918?)
"Woodend"
R.R.1, Allandale, Ont.

Well James, Me boy: down on your knees and give great gobs of thanks to Allah! – sing His praises…we have a car waiting [for] us on the Algoma central!!! A car to live in, eat in and work out of. They will move us about as we desire…Your only real essentials as I see it now, are blankets (lots of them), warm clothes and sketching outfit. I also suggest a rig that will enable you to keep dry and sketch in the rain.

We leave Toronto the evening of Tues. the 10th or Wed. the 11th of Sept., arrive Soo next day – board our car and stay therein and thereout for three weeks or so, having supplies, mail etc. left us by passing trains every second day or so…

✧✧✧

(1918 or 1919?)
"Woodend"
R.R.1, Allandale, Ont.

Dear Jim,
…once we leave the Soo and commence climbing into that paradise you will forget entirely to give your health or state of mind even a passing thought – just give up to drinking in gorgeousness with your eyes, sweet woodsy sounds with your ears and crisp, clear air with your lungs, God bless you!…

The following excerpts are taken from Algoma letters sent by Frank (later Franz) Johnston to his wife. They are included courtesy of the National Archives of Canada, Ottawa, Mary Bishop Rodrik – Franz Johnston Collection (R320).

✧✧✧

Sept 29/19
Hubert A.C.R.

My Dear Girl [Mrs. Johnston]
…You could not possibly imagine how quiet and lonely [lovely?] it is here with the chaps out and not a sound but the fire in the stove and the wind in the trees outside.

✧✧✧

Oct 1/19
Hubert A.C.R.

My Dear
This has been one grand day, in fact we have had two fine days in succession, and it naturally makes us jubilant.

All the reds have practically gone but the birch trees are hanging on to their leaves. The forests are one mass of gold, dotted with the deep green spruce spiring up like cathedrals…

Mac is doing some very nice work very much finer than what he did last year. He and I had a little picnic today. We took the jigger (you know that means hand car) and went down to the Montreal Falls where the big trestle is – but we did not go over it – we went under and down by the falls and I think made one of the best sketches I have made up here…

It was very wonderful down there sketching by the gorgeous falls pounding down – <u>it</u> or they seemed to fascinate you and the great roar of the water withal being a bright sunny day it made the place like an enchanted land. Mac fairly beemed [*sic*] with it. I think I must have beemed a little myself it was beyond description.

✧✧✧

Oct 6/19
Hubert

My Dear
...All the waterproofs, umbrellas, and weather proofs have proven their worth on a dozen occasions and many a sketch of mine has been saved by my oilskin slicker and the umbrella; there have been times when it seemed as if there never had been any fine weather...

I was counting my sketches just before I started to write this letter and would you believe it – fifty-seven –...the reason is that we know where to find the stuff this year and it saves a lot of looking around.... I think one of the sketches I made today is possibly one of the best I have made up here, a very simple decorative type of thing but a good size 21 x 25.

Tomorrow we move on [to] the next to last leg of our trip. Batchewanna is the place, and I hope to get some good stuff there, particularly fine foreground stuff. The detail in this country suggests a thousand themes for decoration, and of course the ensemble is equally as beautiful as the detail...

In parts of the country now the leaves are practically all off and you can see far into the woods, and it gives you an entirely different idea of the country...

Yesterday, Lawren and I went up the lake and stayed most [of] the day on a little island, of course we took our lunch, which consisted of a pickle sandwich and a can of pears, and it tasted fine up there sitting on the rocks with lovely spruce trees towering up above us and the lake dotted with islands below. The hills are just a mass of purple and gold...

The following letters written by J.E.H. MacDonald in 1918 and the section of his diary from 1919, once in the collection of Thoreau MacDonald, have been included here through the courtesy of a private collector.

✧✧✧

Monday Thury. Sept.? '18
Canyon Station, Mile 113, Algoma Central Ry.

Tell Thoreau there are plenty of moose here. Lawren and the old man chased one down the track on Saturday –

Dear Joan: – Frank has just gone singing down the railway track, in the tail end of a little procession comprising the Dr. [Dr. MacCallum] & Lawren, led by "Woofie" as we call the dog. ("Woofie" is his commonest name, but he is often addressed by Lawren as "you poor old fish." After that "Mutt" is probably the name he gets and deserves most. For "Woofie" is not distinguished in intellect. He supports his dignity on his ancestry, & has more blue blood than grey matter. Lawren tells of a little girl who came to play with the children, & when the formidable "Prince" (which is "Woofie's" real christened name) approached her, she said "O, but it was a dear nice kind "Woofie".– go 'way, go 'way, go 'way" – the fear of "nice, kind "Woofie," increasing as he came nearer. But Woofie has his merits. He has no fussiness, & only quiet dignified anxieties. He was howling the other day when Lawren had left him here, & at night there was some more howling down the tract as though he had been heard by some wolfish relations of his.) Well, as I said, or began to say, the folks have departed, leaving the canyon to Ichi Manitou & me. They are headed for a chain of idyllic waterfalls, three or four miles off, & as I don't feel like tackling that walk, I am keeping house alone. I expect to go down there this afternoon, when our neighbor at the section house, old Sam Corbeil, French-Canadian railway man & trapper is going to take me on his "jigger."

I will not attempt to describe this country for you, as I haven't a great flow of language at present. Perhaps that will come as usual when I get back & talk as usual after a trip. But the country is certainly all that Lawren & the Dr. said about it. It is a sort of little Yosemite, full of "Glacier? Points" and other notable features. It is a land after Dante's heart. The canyon is like a winding way to the lower regions & last night, when a train went through just at dusk, with the fireman stoking up, the light of the fire stirring on the smoke clouds, it was easy to imagine his Satanic majesty taking a drive through his domain. I had walked a little distance up the canyon, and the effect was eerie enough to make me speed up for home. The great perpendicular rocks seemed to overhang as though they might fall any minute & the dark Agawa moving quietly through it all had an uncanny snakiness. But yesterday was a dull & rainy day. On a fine day, such as this, the canyon seems to lead *upwards* & has all the attributes of an imagined Paradise, excepting perhaps anything in the way of meadows. There are beautiful waterfalls on all sides & the finest trees, spruce, elm & pine. It is a Shelly like kind of place & certainly would make a great background for gods and goddesses either white or red.

I think the most impressive sight I have had on this trip was a view of lake Superior from a place about eight miles from here, on the way up. The railway is there within about 4 miles of the lake & probably 1500 feet above it, commanding a wonderful view of craggy hills, waterfalls & the winding Agawa. I have never seen anything so impressive, as the half-revealed extensiveness of the lake. It certainly was <u>Superior</u> in all ways. There was a haziness in the air which merged the horizon with the sky & that smooth glimmering infinity of waters was like a glimpse of God himself. A few large islands could be seen & great rocky shores stooping grandly to the water. One of the islands was 12 miles long, the brakeman told me, but it looked like a crumb on the table. I have not quite assimilated this experience yet. It is something to be quiet about & think over. It reminds one of Paul, being caught up & hearing unutterable things. It seems hardly credible to such a creeper as myself that such things could be seen in the body & yet there it was, & it looked as though it would always be.

I would like to tell you about our experiences in coming here, but must wait. I intend to try to write it down some time. The whole thing reminded me of Conrad's 'Typhoon' in miniature. I have a great sympathy with the tramps who ride in freight cars, after it. Am glad to say that I am feeling much better. All of us are working full time especially L. & F. They are both "dippy" as they express it, about the country. Admiration & surprise are so common that we have one word to save trouble. It is adapted from the name of my watch "Linto." So a "Genuine Linto" is a real fine view. In looking at anything we merely remark "Linto" and let it go at that. The leaves are hardly turned at all but are beginning. The whole country is green & rich as the Highlands. I hope everything is alright at home.

With love to Thoreau & all.

Yours, J.

I don't know when we will leave here, but if you are writing you might address as above.

✧✧✧

Hubert. Sept. 24, '18

Dear Joan: – We are about to begin another stage of our journey by leaving here this aft. Today we enter on the third week of the trip. And it has certainly been a busy time. Have got 26 sketches up to now, & Frank & Lawren more than that. The weather is first rate, quite warm & summery yesterday with the black flies busy on my noble brow, bright again today with frost this mrg. & a fresh breeze from the further north coming down the lake. We have seen some great country in this section, especially on Sunday, when we visited the falls of the Montreal river, about 3 miles away. An old man who watches the big bridge there came up here & took me down on his "pede." The other fellows went down on the "pede" belonging [to] this section, & we had our lunch in the old man's cabin, he doing the host by making us a backwoods cup of cocoa each. He is an old Irishman named Brandon, with part dreams of mineral wealth from his claims near at hand. He talks exactly like Mrs. Caldwell & one could easily imagine the old lady round while listening to him. He showed us the sights of his place & they were little short of Niagara in grandeur. The falls are tremendous & though I did not get down below them, as the bank[s] are about 150 ft high & the foot of the fall considerably lower than that, I got two sketches of the upper falls, which are fairly successful. The whole Montreal river is very impressive. Looking at it from the Ry. trail on our way home, we felt that we could understand something of the feeling of the early Canadian explorers. The whole scene seemed so primeval & unspoiled & and the great broad river another St. Lawrence waiting for discoverers. I went to the place again yesterday, & while working there a couple of photographers came along. They were making views for a Montreal firm. & took a picture right where I sat. I arranged with them to get a print. They told me that they had been in a good many parts of Canada, but had never seen anything better, even Trinity Cape on the Saguenay they thought inferior to a great rocky bluff rising out of the river. I was interested in watching their reckless climbing & placing of their camera, on steep sloping rocks & dangerous ledges without any cautions apparently. And the color was a positive burlesque & carnival. It would make you drunk. But I must hurry along.

We expect to leave for home about a week from today. So we shall probably be back in the old spot again next Wednesday. There may be hindrances but we are planning that way. Until then I hope all the problems will sleep peacefully. They don't seem to have any existence here at all, & I wish they would "contining(?) in the same."

Yours in haste.

J.

As we have this place all to ourselves, Frank & L. are having a great time yelling anything that comes into their heads. Frank is singing & in between bars, imitating crows & giving wolf howls. We seem to be the only people on earth at this minute. It was quite startling to see a lady on a passenger train that went through a few minutes ago.

✧✧✧

J. MacD.

Algoma Trip. Sept 17, '19
[property T. MacD.]

We left the Sou on Wed morning Sept. 18, attached to the regular passenger train, and arrived at Canyon the same afternoon. Heavy rains all the way. The few hunter's camp stations on the way forlorn & sodden, a man getting off the train at one place & running through the pouring rain with a baby in his arms. A backwoods family going from one little station to another on a visit. The children all tied up with bows and dressed in their best. Very short intervals in ages. Acquainted all along the line, & calling from the windows as to their destination, "Going to Mckatima." had dinner on the train with A.Y.J. At Batchawana began to renew definite impressions of last year's visit. The water in rivers much lower, which gave the place a different character, and made the river more picturesque as it increases the sand bars and the number of rapids. At Montreal River the train was run very slowly across the bridge, so that party in the manager's private car might get a good look at the falls. "The Wild River" tamer than usual, but with enough…with…Ferry. Was glad to find that one's old impression of the country was pleasantly renewed.

Selected Bibliography

Duval, Paul. *The Tangled Garden*. Toronto: Cerebrus/Prentice-Hall, 1978.

Eisenberg, Evan. *The Ecology of Eden*. Toronto: Random House of Canada, 1998.

Harris, Lawren. "The Group of Seven in Canadian History," *Canadian Historical Association: Report of the Annual Meting held at Victoria and Vancouver, 16–19 June 1948*. Toronto: University of Toronto Press, 1948, pages 28–38.

Harris, Lawren. *The Story of the Group of Seven*. Toronto: Rous and Mann Press, 1964.

Hill, Charles C. *The Group of Seven: Art for a Nation*. Ottawa and Toronto: National Gallery of Canada and McClelland & Stewart,1995.

Housser, F.B. *A Canadian Art Movement: The Story of the Group of Seven*. Toronto: Macmillan, 1926.

Jackson, A.Y. "Box-car Days in Algoma 1919–20." *Canadian Art* 14 (Summer 1957), pages 136–41.

Jackson, A.Y. *A Painter's Country: The Autobiography of A.Y. Jackson*. Toronto, Vancouver: Clarke, Irwin & Company, 1958.

Jessup, Lynda. "The Group of Seven and the Tourist Landscape in Western Canada, or the More Things Change . . ." *Journal of Canadian Studies* 37 (Spring 2002), pages 144–79.

Larisey, Peter. *Light for a Cold Land*. Toronto: Dundurn Press, 1993.

MacDonald, J.E.H. "The Canadian Spirit in Art." *The Statesman* 35 (22 March 1919), pages 6–7.

MacDonald, J.E.H. "A.C.R. 10557." *The Lamps* (December 1919), pages 33–39.

MacLennan, Hugh. *Rivers of Canada*. Toronto: Macmillan of Canada, 1974.

Martinsen, Hanna. "The Scandinavian Impact on the Group of Seven's Vision of the Canadian Landscape." *Konsthistorisk Tidskrift* LIII (1984), pages 1–17.

Murray, Joan. *Lawren Harris: An Introduction to His Life and Art*. Toronto: Firefly Books, 2003.

Reid, Dennis, and Charles C. Hill. *Tom Thomson*. Toronto: Art Gallery of Ontario, 2002.

Robertson, Nancy E. "Introduction." *J.E.H. MacDonald, R.C.A., 1873–1932*. Toronto: Art Gallery of Toronto, 1965.

Stacey, Robert, and Hunter Bishop. *J.E.H. MacDonald: Designer: An Anthology of Graphic Design, Illustration and Lettering*. Ottawa: Archives of Canadian Art, an imprint of Carleton University Press, 1996.

Taylor, David G. *Gallery Lambton: Group of Seven Collection*. Sarnia: Gallery Lambton, 2003.

Varley, Christopher. *F.H. Varley*. Edmonton: The Edmonton Art Gallery, 1981.

Wadland, John H. "Great Rivers, Small Boats: Landscape and Canadian Historical Culture," in John S. Marsh and Bruce W. Hodgins (eds.). *Changing Parks: The History, Future and Cultural Context of Parks and Heritage Landscapes*. Toronto: Natural Heritage, 1998, pages 1–33.

Illustration Credits

Agnes Etherington Art Centre, Queen's University 39

Art Gallery of Hamilton 47, 91

Art Gallery of Nova Scotia, Halifax 87

Art Gallery of Ontario, Toronto 13, 17, 77, 95, 105

Gallery Lambton, Sarnia 51

Hart House, University of Toronto 61, 73, 107

Heffel Fine Art Auction House 117

Imperial Oil Limited 57

McMichael Canadian Art Collection, Kleinburg 8, 31, 33, 37, 49, 55, 63, 65, 67, 71, 75, 93, 97, 115

National Gallery of Canada, Ottawa 7, 53, 59, 69, 89, 99, 101, 103, 109, 111, 113

Tom Thomson Memorial Art Gallery, Owen Sound 35, 81

The Thomson Collection, Toronto 43, 45

Varley Gallery, Markham 83

Private Collector, Toronto 79

Private Collector, Toronto viii, 5, 15, 19

Private Collector, Winnipeg 85

The Winnipeg Art Gallery 41

Acknowledgements

In preparing this text, I have been greatly helped by curators, registrars, and collection managers across Canada. I would like to thank the following individuals and public and private galleries in particular for their help with information, the location of works, and supplying photographs: Annabel F. Hanson of the Agnes Etherington Art Centre, Queen's University, Kingston; Christine Braun of the Art Gallery of Hamilton; Judy E. Dietz of the Art Gallery of Nova Scotia, Halifax; Laura Brown, Barry Simpson, Liana Radvak, and the helpful staff of the Edward P. Taylor Research Library and Archives of the Art Gallery of Ontario, Toronto; David G. Taylor of the Gallery Lambton, Sarnia; Robert C.S. Heffel of the Heffel Fine Art Auction House, Vancouver and Toronto; Janine Butler and Linda Morita of the McMichael Canadian Art Collection, Kleinburg; Eve Kotyk of the Mendel Art Gallery, Saskatoon; Anne Goddard and Michael MacDonald of the National Archives of Canada, Ottawa; Sharon Odell and Shawn Boisvert of the National Gallery of Canada, Ottawa; Christy Telford and Kelly Lisle of the Tom Thomson Art Gallery, Owen Sound; Christopher Varley of Toronto and Estelle Guthro of the Winnipeg Art Gallery. In the gallery where I am Director Emerita, The Robert McLaughlin Gallery in Oshawa, Olexander Wlasenko and Holly McClellan generously offered assistance. In the gallery where I am Adjunct Curator, the Varley Art Gallery of Markham in Unionville, John Ryerson assisted with information and a photograph of a work for the book. I thank them for their help.

Joan Murray,
Oshawa

The main text is set in Monotype Fournier. It is a Transitional, or Neo-Classical typeface, originally designed c. 1740 by Pierre Simon Fournier, Paris. It was recut and released in 1926 by Monotype, England. The credits are set in FFMeta, designed 1985–91 by Erik Spiekerman, Berlin.
Separations by Quadratone Graphics, Limited.
Printed by Friesens Printers.